BACKPACK HIKING:
The First Steps

BACKPACK HIKING:
The First Steps

Richard Eggert

Illustrated by
Tony and Jo Ann Sandoval

STACKPOLE BOOKS

BACKPACK HIKING: THE FIRST STEPS
Copyright © 1977 by
Richard Eggert

Published by
STACKPOLE BOOKS
Cameron and Kelker Streets
P.O. Box 1831
Harrisburg, Pa. 17105

Published simultaneously in Don Mills, Ontario,
Canada by Thomas Nelson & Sons, Ltd.

Printed in the U.S.A.

Library of Congress Cataloging in Publication Data

Eggert, Richard.
    Backpack hiking.

    Includes index.
    1. Backpacking. I. Title.
GV199.6.E36   796.5'1   76–56813
ISBN 0–8117–2256–2

Contents

10. APPRECIATION AND ETHICS 183
• the community • animals • birds • fishing •
swimming • side trips • and now, a word about
our product

Introduction

If there is one thing that characterizes our western civilization and separates it from other ways of being human, it is our arrogant and often hostile attitude toward nature and the wilderness.

Throughout the five thousand years of western social and technological evolution we have sought first to insulate civilization from the forces of nature, then to exploit her, and finally to occupy her like a defeated nation.

Indeed, the milestones of European science, from Aristotle to Einstein, have been attempts to unlock the secrets of natural law and turn them against nature and the wilderness. The basic premise of the modern Baconian scientific method, which we have been following blindly for the past four hundred years, is to better the human condition by utilizing the tools of natural philosophy.

Those living in comfort and luxury today are the

heirs of this dichotomy between nature and humanity. We are the children of technology, born of science and the industrial revolution. Our grandparents were natural philosophy and alchemy which descended from theology. From these roots we inherited the notion that the wilderness was an enemy to be feared and defeated and that the laws of nature were our weapons. Man, according to the beliefs of our great-grandfathers, was born, and lost his innocence in the wild Garden of Eden. And man, according to the wisdom of our ancestors, should take revenge on his natal place by regarding it with suspicion and loathing, entering it only to conquer or raze.

This historical path through the wilderness began when western peoples came down from the foothills and forests to march together. It is now a four-lane, asphalt-and-concrete-paved highway which nearly covers the globe and has buried most of the wilderness. We have nearly succeeded in domesticating the planet.

Human beings are now the masters of everything they behold. In the United States we live in the security of cities paved wall-to-wall and suburbs connected to one another by coast-to-coast super highways. We have checkerboarded the valleys and plains with the means to feed ourselves. Even the foothills of our forests are rendered into timber croplands with neatly squared-off blocks and even-age tree stands waiting for the saws.

Where there are no crops or commercial forests, there are great holes where we have picked, prodded, and scraped for the earth's minerals. Our great rivers, the lifeblood of our society a hundred years ago, are putrid from our wastes and swollen by dams built to sate our lust for power.

Fewer than five percent of the people living in the United States make their living through direct contact with nature's skin. The rest of us go about our abstract and abstracted "civilized arts," remote from the land and safe from "bloody nature, fang, and claw," content with allowing the complex organization of society to see to our basic needs.

We are becoming like terminal patients in a hospital ward with an army of orderlies seeing to our security, sanitation, and feeding. We are safe from the dangers outside—the savage wilderness and its orderly, but sometimes harsh, natural laws—and the only dues we pay for all this comfort is unquestioning compliance with another set of social laws.

Many people were born, live, and will die within these walls, never seeing beyond them. And that is a pity because our grandfathers, who left us the fear-legacy of the wilderness, knew there was something out there other than toil, terror, and triumph. There was also, as Henry David Thoreau put it a century ago, "redemption."

The wilderness has always been a handy place for saviors, saints, prophets, and eccentrics to prove their vision, mettle, or madness. And this is the fundamental paradox of western man: We have always feared and avoided the wilderness as a place of danger and evil, but at the same time have recognized that without it there would be no reliable testing ground for our bodies and souls. Without wilderness we lose the possibility of genius or salvation. If we cannot pit our own animal natures against or with the wild forces, we soon become too civilized; like a race of domesticated and docile cows.

And today, even the most sophisticated citizens of our packaged society sometimes hear the echo of wild, distant drums. It can be the rhythm of any number of natural forces: The roaring of the sea, the sweet song of a trout stream, the brooding chorus of the mountains, or just the laughing of birds or the whispering of trees in the wind. These primal symphonies stir us with fantasies and longings with which we are no longer equipped to deal. We call it spring fever or daydreaming and try to ignore it. If it begins to dominate us, we are called idle or indolent and society brings us quickly back into line with the reality of our responsibilities and our terror of failure.

But for a moment there was a crack in the wall—our civilized veneer. We saw something out there that was beautiful, frightening, and compelling. Some people deny the beauty and compulsion by turning on the television or going bowling. Others find safe ways of probing the ground on the other side of this metaphysical barrier we have erected. They go walking in the woods, up north hunting once a year, or get their feet wet in a trout stream and feel the primal chill from a safe distance. These short reconnaissance trips into the wilds are only tentative, and it is easy to retreat back into the security of concrete and ordered civilization.

Those who reject this curiosity, or sublimate it by taking guided tours on the edge of the wilderness, are following an indelibly imprinted behavior pattern. For them, getting both feet into the wilderness (backpacking or mountaineering), would be a terrifying and traumatic experience.

There are others—many, many others—who seem to have a genuine vocation for the wilds. They feel that an important part of themselves belongs in the wilderness, and guided tours on the fringe are not enough to quell their urge. They are going to have to take their first steps into a new experience.

It is for these people that this book was prepared. Those who already know they have a destiny in the mountains on lightly trodden paths, and don't need any coaxing. They need only advice and direction for taking their first backpacking trip, and I hope this book will help.

If you are among these, you have probably already heard that stalking off into the wilds offers a combination of titillating experiences. That, for instance, it is nearly as pleasurable as sex, is a spiritual revelation, builds strong bodies and keen minds, is almost as intellectually stimulating as existentialism, stirs long-repressed and valuable instincts, and involves a glorious and bottomless collection of new and interesting toys. All of these pre-suppositions are true, to a degree, but don't be disappointed if you return from your first trip without any divine revelations or infinite wisdom. The inspirations and infinites come slowly and are cumulative, so do be patient.

You are probably also aware, since you have spent money to buy this book, and a few minutes to see if it is worth reading, that backpacking is not a church picnic. Even simple overnight or weekend trips require a lot of planning and some expense, and you realize the price for the possibility of seeing something worthwhile out there may be a lot of sweat and toil, and perhaps some pain. But if you are really interested, you will find what you are looking for and will know it when you see or feel it.

CHAPTER ONE

The Groundwork

WHY HIKE?

There are any number of reasons for going hiking, but until recently backpacking was not usually considered among them.

Backpacking and hiking have traditionally been considered a means to an end. In the past, prospectors, foresters, surveyors, explorers, geologists, and anthropologists used backpacking as tools of their trades. Professionals in these disciplines were often called to remote areas, and packing a rucksack or crude wood frame with domestic essentials was frequently the only way of getting there.

During the 19th century, hauling a camp on the back became a way of pursuing sports in the untrodden wilderness. Mountain climbers, hunters, fishermen, and amateur naturalists began following faint game trails to reach areas that challenged their sporting skill and imagination during their leisure time. A generation ago, most people who wandered the hills were still looking for something beyond the trail. They were seeking virgin lakes with innocent fish, untrodden ridges with plentiful game, isolated mountains still unclimbed, sights and sounds that few had sensed.

Today, however, the trail and the trek have developed into an end unto themselves for thousands of backpackers. There are still those who seek other things at the end of the trail and, indeed, most overnight hikers are equipped to catch a fish, take a picture, or explore a hill at the end of the journey.

But most of today's hikers sweat the trails and swat the mosquitoes because of some personal fascination with the process of getting their jaded bodies from point A to point B and back. There is a gestalt whole about backpacking—the sights, the smells, the sounds, the strain, the tempering, the fish, the game, the lakes, the mountains and hills, and the swelling of the soul—that makes the experience not only worthwhile but something to be cherished.

All this may sound a little daft. No doubt people have been burned at the stake or committed as incorrigible lunatics for less bizarre pursuits. After all, we live in a pragmatic, productive society which has always venerated the careful and judicious use of personal energy. Why, then, should anyone carry a fifty-pound pack up a hill, spend several days, and return without any material gain?

The answer is in the deed. There can be no rational reason for such irrational phenomena. You must try it for yourself and, after doing so, if you still ask the question, you will probably never find the answer.

But you don't have to be a purist to enjoy backpacking. If the idea of doing little more than putting

one foot in front of the other and returning empty-
handed from the wilds does not intrigue you, maybe you ought to think of backpacking as a way of
further developing an avocation you already have. If
you are one who goes fishing, for instance, getting a
day or two off the beaten shore will probably produce
fish that bite more readily.

FINDING A TRAIL

In choosing a site for your first backpack outing, several considerations should be examined: The
time available; the amount of money you can afford
to experiment with; the micro-type of experience you
are seeking; and the relative difficulty of the hike.

We are assuming you have never been overnight-
hiking before or that your only experience was
under tightly controlled and equipped situations
such as Boy Scout camps or dude ranch excursions.
Therefore, your first solo flight (regardless of
whether you are by yourself or not), should be in the
nature of a shakedown. When a ship is launched it is
usually taken for a short cruise, to find out how well
it floats, and to tighten up all the loose ends. A
prospective backpacker, like a ship, probably has
all the right equipment—legs that work together,
strong lungs for air, adequate muscles and a mind
that is capable of making rational decisions—but
should test these and the specialized equipment
before going on any protracted odysseys.

An overnight or weekend excursion of three to six
miles would be an ideal shakedown hike. The length
of the hike should be determined by the relative difficulty of the trail and the grade. Well-manicured
trails and grown-over logging roads are much easier
and faster than thin hiking trails and game trails.

Steep grades make both the coming and the going
more difficult and tiresome, so take them into account as you plan your outing.

Another important consideration in planning a
shakedown is travel time and expense. It would
hardly be feasible to travel from New York City to
Glacier National Park in Montana to spend your
first night in the woods, unless you can integrate the
journey into other plans. Most states, including and
perhaps especially New York, have ample trails and
wild public lands for a maiden voyage, and most
have the peripheral attractions such as fishing, to
offer incentive for an overnight hike.

Thoreau once answered an inquiry about his
worldliness by noting he had "travelled much in
Concord." It seems to be one of the curses of modern
man to be myopic to the forest that grows around the
jungles we live in. We think that because we have
conquered and salted the lands around New York
City or Kalamazoo, Michigan, we have to go far
afield to rid our bodies and souls of our own civilizing influence. But, in fact, New York has some of the
most charming wild lands in the nation within half
a day's drive from the city, and Kalamazoo is virtually surrounded by richly beautiful rolling hills
and meadows. Neither of these places, nor most
other areas in the country, have the vast and mysterious majesty of the Rocky Mountains, but you
don't really need quite that much physical and
metaphysical elbow room for your first overnight
trip.

If you look around your community or make inqui-
ries, you will probably find there is an ideal
thumbnail wilderness within a day's drive. Friends
who hunt, fish, or backpack normally know some

out-of-the-way undeveloped lands nearby, or you can ask at nearly any sporting goods store or mountaineering shop. You might also contact the nearest office of the state fish and game or conservation department about areas and special regulations (such as fire, fish size and limit, or specimen collecting), in your area or state.

Good libraries generally have a large collection of topographical maps of the area or state and it might help to look through these for likely places. When you do finally select a place for your shakedown, you will probably want to purchase your own map (or maps), of the area so take note of the quadrangle description given in the lower right-hand corner. To order, send this description, along with $1.50 to the U.S. Geological Survey in either Denver, Colorado, 80225 (for maps west of the Rockies), or Washington, D.C., 20242 (for maps east of the Rockies).

If you have difficulty deciding which maps to buy or how to go about purchasing them, contact either your county surveyor, lands commission office, or planning office. These people work with "topo" maps on a day-to-day basis and should be able to help with just about any problems or questions you may have.

Another and perhaps the most interesting way of picking your first backpacking trail is to take weekend drives through the country. If you discover a likely set of hills or forests, ask around to find out how much contiguous wild lands there are and if there is any restriction against hiking or camping. You might even attempt an exploratory jaunt into the area to see if it feels right. When you get back home, double-check on the desirability and accessibility of the area with friends who are interested in the outdoors, or your state conservation department.

It may take you a while to find your trail, but looking around helps foster anticipation for the hike and
familiarization with the lay of the land.

When you have checked out your site thoroughly,
buy topo maps covering the extent of your hike and
campgrounds to familiarize yourself with the bend
of the trail and the characteristics of the land. Later
we will see how to translate the wiggly lines on topo
maps into a language of the land. Study this language carefully, learn the tongue fluently and con-
verse often with the maps of your trail.

PLANNING A SHAKEDOWN HIKE

After you and the map have learned to get along—
and you will, because maps virtually have a per-
sonality of their own with dimensions that jump out
at you as your acquaintance deepens—let it tell you
more or less where to go and how to get there. Trails
are marked in dashed lines on topo maps. On a 7½–
minute scale quadrangle (the most common map), a
mile is represented by a little over 2½ inches. For a
relatively leisurely trek up a rough trail, allow yourself at least one hour for every mile. Add to this
another hour for every 1,000 feet of vertical climb,
and you have a rough idea of the distance you can
travel within the time allotted.

Using this formula, a five-mile hike will take
about five hours on the level, or six hours with a
1,000-foot climb.

Now find a desirable camping spot—a lake or
streamside if you are piscatorially inclined, or a site
beside a rustling rill if you are just looking—and
find out if you can make it there within the amount
of time you will have to hike. Remember not to
extend your allotted trail time till sundown just be-

cause it is a convenient reference. Allow yourself at least an hour for laying out camp and dinner and another half hour for good measure. If your projected camping site is within the allotted time, you are in business. If not, find another suitable place for your first night and plan to exercise the option of spending a second night at the original site.

CONDITIONING

Now that you have the route and the site fixed, you are ready to acquire your gear and start packing. Or are you?

Everyday conditioning, unfortunately, is quite subjective. You may walk from the train depot or parking lot to the office every day, play a fast round of handball or tennis once a week and consider yourself fit for the Olympics. There is no reliable objective criteria to judge your conditioning unless you are stressing your body in ways similar to uphill climbing.

It is probably safe to say that you are not in as good shape as you are going to wish you were after a couple of miles on a rocky trail. The only solution is to whip yourself into the best possible condition before you reach the trailhead and worry about recriminations two miles up the path.

Conditioning should include general health and, if you have a history of organic problems or suspect a situation might be developing, see a doctor and get his recommendation on your planned trip. If all is well with your vitals, then you can concentrate on tuning up the drive train.

The best form of around-town conditioning is jogging. Slow running is probably also the least entertaining and most difficult exercise to continue on a regular basis.

Many mountaineers and hikers begin jogging in the early spring when the weather is cool and the ground clear of snow and vegetation. This vernal ritual helps purge the lungs of winter's excesses, and wakes up sedentary muscles.

You may want to start out with a slow half-mile trot up and down a mild grade. Time the runs and gradually increase the speed over a week. During the second week slow down the pace and stretch the jog over a mile, which should include one mild hill and one moderately steep slope. Creep up the speed on successive runs so you can show yourself some progress. Usually by the third day your thigh muscles will be so sore you will be running stiff-legged most of the way and have to take a second or third place in the race against indolence.

At any rate, timing jogs is the only way I find I can maintain interest. Progress is slow and sometimes uneven, but two or three seconds off the clock provides enough of self-approbation to keep me running until the weather is fine enough to get into the hills regularly. This also happens to correspond to the raising of the nets and the start of spring tennis.

Tennis, as well as squash, handball, paddleball and other forms of competitive sport that require constant movement, are nearly as good as jogging for getting into hiking trim and they are considerably more compelling. The heat of competition is enough to overcome human sloth and, indeed, you do a lot of fast moving in a hard set. A friend of mine carried a pedometer calibrated for a short stride during a three-set match. He found he had moved the equivalent of six and a half miles in two hours. Those miles on the courts every day can really help shrink the distance on the trails.

Modern living requires enormous amounts of routine daily travel. It is safe to say that nearly everybody in the United States today moves scores of horizontal miles every day and perhaps thousands of vertical feet. The problem is, most of this vast distance is spanned in machines—trains or cars to work or shopping—elevators to carry us up in the morning and back down at night. If only a fraction of this distance were walked or climbed every day, we would probably be among the most fit people in the world. Because people are required to make these daily treks anyway, why not get some good out of them? Walk instead of taking a cab; climb stairs rather than use the elevator; use the ramp instead of the escalator; walk home from the station or between stores; cover as much of your daily routine on your feet as possible.

Food and eating habits are another vital part of conditioning that are often either neglected or distorted. If you are carrying an extra twenty pounds on your body, you are obviously going to have a lot more trouble with an additional twenty-five-pound pack. Conversely, if you crash-diet to become an anemic beanpole, you are not going to have the strength necessary to sustain a comfortable pace on the trail.

The solution, of course, is to eat right. Ample, nutritious meals along with sensible exercise will keep you in running trim better than excesses in dieting or bone-grinding exercises.

And remember, while you are honing yourself into a sleek long-distance athlete, you will probably have companions on your shakedown hike. A hiking party is like a convoy of ships, the fastest and sleekest must slow to the pace of the slowest and most portly. If you intend to make your first excursion a family affair, see to it that spouse and offspring are eating as well as you and getting a commensurate amount of miles on their legs and lungs.

With families it is easy to get into shape together; you can simply share wholesome fare and organize a regimen of exercise. With friends it is a different matter. You can't monitor their eating habits, and dragging them out of the house for a Saturday morning jog may end the friendship before the hike even starts. If your prospective hiking companions are relatively serious about probing into the realm of nature, you should be able to convince them that some minimal conditioning is necessary. Challenge them to a game of tennis so that both you and they can assess their relative degree of conditioning.

In the meantime, while the rubber on your stomach is being converted to a ripple on your legs and the site of your shakedown hike is shaping up, there are some material problems that must be considered before you go off into the wilds for a night.

CHAPTER TWO

Planning Equipment Needs

A lot of thought and sweat has gone into the evolution and manufacture of backpacking and camping equipment and each hiker should devote some thought and a little perspiration to his individual equipment needs.

Modern backpacking gear is a material paradox: it is at once lovely, light, sleek, and comfortable and it is also expensive, heavy, hard-to-fit, confusing, and awkward. Today's synthetic lightweight materials and minutely refined manufacturing techniques have chopped ten pounds off the average backpack load of twenty years ago. But even if the average summertime weekend pack weight has been dropped to twenty or thirty pounds, that is still enough dead weight to make a long, uphill grade uncomfortable.

When you get to your first camp you will find that a five-pound, two-man tent is not a living room, and if you are confined to it for any time, your outing can become an ordeal. Most beginning hikers, and even some seasoned veterans, have a hard time adjusting their sleeping habits to confining mummy-style sleeping bags. In spite of the best modern synthetic weaves and waterproof coatings, if it rains hard enough, almost everything will get wet. There are ways of avoiding these problems by buying equipment wisely, packing it carefully, and pitching it sensibly.

Virtually hundreds of small-to-modest backpacking outfitters are marketing highly streamlined equipment today. Most of this gear evolved from the tough, heavy, and spartan government issue of the Second World War.

The army, in turn, borrowed liberally from equipment designed for pioneer alpine mountaineering. Most of the basic design forms found in modern equipment were developed by these prewar mountaineers. The standard A-frame tent using two angled poles at either end evolved then and is still the foundation of most lightweight tents. The old tents were made of cotton canvas or duck and weighed three or four times as much as the modern nylon version, but the form was there.

The mountaineers of two generations ago also developed the standard baffled mummy bags filled with down still in use. These bags had cotton or silk covers and could be compressed into small containers for packing. They were warm for their weight, even if they were not exactly uptown sleeping accommodations.

These hardy mountain climbers also developed the first kerosene, alcohol, and white gas stoves to cook with above the timberline. They were light, fuel-efficient and, basically, the same stoves you will be considering today.

About the only piece of backpacking mountaineering equipment that has changed radically since World War II is the backpack itself. In the old days hikers had a choice of the heavy, cumbersome, and anatomically gruesome rucksack or the confining and uncomfortable packboard. Rucksacks were internally-framed bags which tended to load heavily on shoulders and the small of the back; with twenty or thirty pounds of gear they could mold an uphill hiker into a more or less permanent swayback. Packboards could carry heavier loads without any permanent damage, mostly because they suspended the upper portion of the hiker's body in a kind of mobile traction. A day with a packboard on your back could do wonders for your posture but made stooping over to light the evening fire an ordeal.

Today's packs are descendants of the pack frame with some interesting features from the concept of the rucksack. They can be carried a long way without much pain because they have come a long way in their refinements.

But one advantage of the old spine-tangling packs was the built-in incentive toward material austerity. A rucksacker with a fifteen-pound tent, a five-pound sleeping bag, and five pounds in stoves, waterproofs, and food had just about all he could carry. In fact, many a weekender went up into the hills with nothing more than a light bedroll wrapped in his canvas tarp with a little bit of food wedged in. The idea of a lamp, an extra pair of pants or a portable radio would have been absurd because any one of them could have literally been the straw to break the camel's back.

The rules governing what should be stuffed into a backpack haven't changed over the years even though the weight of the equipment and the design of the pack have changed. You can carry more modern lightweight gear in today's functionally designed packs without breaking your back, but maybe you shouldn't. There are six essential units of equipment: Footwear, bedding, shelter, waterproofs, food and cooking equipment, and something in which to carry all of it.

Footwear. Boots must be comfortable, well supported, strong, highly water-resistant, and surefooted. They may be the most important piece of equipment you will buy, therefore you should shop and spend accordingly. Plan to spend $50 to $65.

Bedding. The basic function of your sleeping bag or bedroll is to keep you warm and cozy at night. You can get away with a heavy wool blanket or stitched-together down comforter but not nearly so well as with a down or synthetic fiber-filled bag. Designate the bag second in importance and also give it number two priority in consideration and cost. Plan to spend $50 to $100.

Shelter. This usually means a tent that can shelter from two to four persons. Here you will have to make a judgment on quality and size, depending on the size and relationship of the anticipated average hiking party and the expected weather conditions. Two-man tents cost between $30 and $200, depending on how slick you want to be. Add another $20 to $40 per extra person. Another alternative is a tarp, normally about ten feet by ten feet. If cleverly strung, this can keep two or three persons reasonably dry in a drizzle. Tarps can be canvas, which is very heavy; nylon, which is ideal; or plastic, which is delicate but inexpensive.

Waterproofs. These are a peripheral essential. If you are carrying either a tarp or a tent with a fly, you can crawl under it to wait out a rain. But if you want to continue hiking during a chilling rain, you will need a waterproof poncho or rainsuit. If you are hiking in warmer climes, you can merely strip down to the bare essentials when it starts to rain, and pack your dry clothes.

Ponchos are probably the most efficient and cheapest form of raingear and are preferred for most backpacking purposes. They can double as a ground cloth or emergency shelter and can even make a handy washtub. They will cost from $3 to $15 depending on material and size.

Food and cooking equipment. An obvious requirement on the trail as well as at home, cooking kits can be either large, party-sized, or small individual units. They cost between $2 and $25 depending on size and complexity. Food costs can be either extremely low or extremely high, depending on your needs or the amount of sacrifices you wish to make. The two important considerations are weight and the well-known phenomena that anything, including your boot, can taste good after a day on the trail.

A pack to put it all in. This is another important piece of equipment you will buy, therefore gauge it accordingly. Packs range in size from tiny 1,500-cubic-inch overnight softpacks to copious 4,500-cubic-inch expedition-frame affairs. Both are extremes, and you should probably aim for something in the middle for an all-around hiking pack. Until recently this meant an aluminum welded frame with a nylon duck sack attached. Within the last five years there has been a lot of development in uniform-weight-distributing softpacks with moderately large capacities. A good frame pack in the 3,500- to 4,000-cubic-inch size costs $40 to $60 while a commensurate weight-bearing softpack costs from about $55 to $70.

These are the basics; you absolutely need to cover each of these needs in gathering your equipment for your shakedown hike. Some of these items can be taken from everyday household equipment, such as dehydrated foods, a wool bedroll, or a tarp. With other things, such as boots and a pack, you would be very ill-advised to go second-class.

The best quality, summer-weight, basic necessities that go into your pack will weigh approximately fifteen pounds. Most adults can hike uphill fairly comfortably with twenty to thirty pounds in a well-fit pack. This leaves you five to fifteen pounds for emergency essentials, electives, and fluff.

The Sierra Club, an environmental, wilderness backpacking and mountaineering group, has devised a list of ten essentials that should be formed into a kind of survival kit for all backpacks. These essentials are: Map of the area; compass; flashlight; sunglasses; extra food; a change of dry clothing; waterproofed matches; candle; pocketknife; and first-aid kit.

Many of these items, such as the knife, sunglasses, map, and compass, you will either want to wear, carry in your pockets or in handy areas of your pack. The others can be wrapped in special watertight packaging and stashed in the bottom of your pack.

Most of these things can be found lying around the house. Others, such as a first-aid kit, should be carefully considered and equipped to meet the potential hazards of hiking in the area you have selected. Later, we will discuss the makeup of a first-aid kit in detail.

We have now added another five to eight pounds to the pack, tipping it in at something over twenty pounds. For some people this is probably about enough, others can comfortably add another five to ten pounds. Be careful about your electives because you are operating under backpacking's first law of higher physics which states, basically: *Whatever you take up, you are at some point going to wish you had left down.* This law can be reduced to an equation for determining the necessity of sundry electives: the utility of a piece of equipment divided by the sum of its weight and the nuisance of caring for it equals the justification for carrying it. Take for example, a camera. Most cameras weigh about three pounds with case and the works. They can also be ruined rather easily by rough handling or dousing. On the positive side of the trade-off, they can graphically log your trip and, in some cases, illustrate phenomena which will truly awe and amaze friends and relatives. Whether or not you give cameras or any other elective a positive utility-nuisance value is largely a personal thing. Just remember that the three-pound camera will have to displace three pounds of other equipment.

There is another austerity formula I rather like and call upon whenever my pack begins to swell too much. It goes like this: *In hiking, what you manage to leave behind is often as important as what you manage to haul along.* Eliminate what you cannot positively justify and you will probably be more comfortable.

BORROWING OR RENTING

Of the six basics, you need absolutely buy only one: your boots. Everything else you can either draw from the household, borrow, or rent.

Using somebody else's gear has several advantages, especially if you are not sure you are going to continue to backpack. The most obvious reason to rent or borrow your first hike's equipment is avoiding or deferring the enormous initial cost of the basics. For the communal basics, the tent, sleeping bag, pack, and waterproofs, you can count on spending more than $200. Renting will cost about one-tenth of that, and borrowing, of course, will cost but a favor.

Another advantage of renting or borrowing is the opportunity to try out different makes and types of equipment. On your first trip you could use one generic form of equipment, say an A-frame tent, down mummy bag, and an external frame pack. On your next trip try a dome tent, synthetic-fiber-filled semirectangular bag, and a softpack (if you can find them). In this way your options, if and when you do decide to buy your own gear, will be more familiar to you, and you should know enough about styles and manufacturers to make a good decision.

One of the problems with leasing is finding an establishment that will rent reasonably good equipment. Most larger towns and cities in recreational areas have stores that specialize in leasing, or sporting goods and climbing stores that will rent gear.

The equipment they rent, however, is usually selected on the basis of durability and price, rather than weight and workmanship. The gear you rent will probably be second-rate, heavy, and possibly somewhat tattered; it will do the job it's supposed to, but that's all.

The remaining alternative—borrowing—assumes you have friends who already backpack. If you are going to borrow their gear, you might as well borrow your friend too. If he is an experienced hiker or climber, his companionship will be invaluable. and even if he is only custodian of the equipment by virtue of a misspent year in the Boy Scouts twenty years ago, he will probably have some idea of how to set it up and use it.

If the equipment is available, but your generous friend is not, be sure to have him check you out on putting it up, taking it down, and repackaging it. If you put a pole through the wall or a stake through the fly of his $250 Himalayan expedition tent, (which isn't hard to do if you don't know how to pitch and stuff them), he will probably damn you to rolling boulders up hills for the rest of time.

And that, of course, is the main disadvantage of borrowing equipment. Light, fine quality backpacking and climbing gear, extremely strong when used properly, is infinitely susceptible to abuse. It is quite easy to ruin both your friend's equipment and his friendship in one short weekend.

SURPLUS

Another possible source for starting equipment is your neighborhood Army-Navy store, but available only sporadically, the equipment is often much more expensive than it ought to be.

A whole generation of backpackers lived their entire outdoor lives under GI olive drab. They slept in scratchy, cramped army feather mummies; under "buddy" shelter halves or sweltering army mountain tents; wore a heavy and clammy army poncho over field fatigues; crammed it all in and struggled under a GI rucksack or field pack; and stumbled and slipped down the slopes in clumsy, smooth-soled combat boots. In those days surplus equipment was cheap, built like a tank, and available almost anywhere.

Nonetheless, army surplus bivouac equipment will get you through your first night or two on the trail, if you can find it and pay for it. Afterwards, you can relegate it to learners or as a monument to your own second battle of Verdun.

There are some compromises that may make army surplus more palatable. Buy a good pair of hiking boots, an inexpensive imported frame sack for about $25, an army feather mummy for $20 to $30, and an army pup- or mountain tent, which will cost another $20 to $30. The investment will be about $125 (including the boots), but your mish-mash will be yours to cherish forever.

EQUIPMENT FOR CHILDREN

If you intend to take your family on your first trek, you are going to have to make some adjustments in planning the equipment. It is probably unwise to take children under eight years of age into the woods for an overnight trip. They won't be able to carry their own weight, will probably drag the rest of the party down with them, and may come out of the hills with a really indelible negative impression of life in the wilderness. Eight-year-olds can be really fine hikers or can be worse than younger children; that is a judgment parents are going to have to make for themselves.

As far as equipment needs are concerned, medium children normally constitute about one-half of an adult. Two eight-to-twelve-year-olds who are used to each other can usually share one roomy sleeping bag (not GI), comfortably. The sum of the two will also constitute the third person in a three-man tent. In other words, children can be regarded as fractions when it comes to planning your camp layout. Two children are equal to one adult, three children equal 1.5 adults, and so on, but there is a hitch: Some young children cannot tolerate close contact with others, and being isolated five miles from nowhere is not the appropriate place to coerce family togetherness. Another weakness in this neat human algebra is the unavoidable fact that small children soon become large children and, if you intend to backpack with your family for some years, this fact must be taken into account when you make your intitial equipment purchase. A three-man tent large enough for mom and dad and two eight-to-ten-year-olds will soon leave one person in the cold. Two-man tents will constitute a little extra burden today (although the extra space can be used for camp storage) but will accommodate growth.

An ample semi-rectangular bag can snuggle two tykes today and another can be added to the family outfit when the first one begins breaking at the seams. An ingenious, although somewhat expensive and time-consuming way of dealing with the expanding problem of children was suggested by Holubar Mountaineering. They manufacture a component, sew-it-yourself, sleeping-bag-kit that is designed to grow with the child. In theory, the lower compartments of the bag are filled with down as the child grows. This principle could be applied to any sew-it-yourself kit sleeping bag.

Another possibility for avoiding annually recurring expenses for bagging children is rotating small bags within your family and with the families of friends. The bag could be purchased jointly by two families with similarly aged children or merely handed down from one child to another. Generally children about twelve years old are ready for an adult sleeping bag, which should last them for awhile.

Keeping kids shod is bad enough under normal conditions, but if you start adding a pair of $35 hiking boots to that bill every year, it will probably tilt the coffers of most families. There is no way of keeping a child's feet from growing and there are few sensible alternatives to good hiking boots for the trail, however, there are a few ways to cut corners.

- If the child is not going to be carrying a pack, or will carry at most a lightly loaded daypack, he can get away with sound street or tennis shoes on a mild hike. If you choose this alternative, avoid areas with lots of loose rock (which can easily turn an unsupported ankle), and solid rock faces (which can be extremely slippery under street shoes).

- Buy the child the $35 boots and have him wear them as street and play shoes.

- You can buy Vibram or lug-type soled play shoes for $15 to $20, which are better than tennis shoes, although they don't really have the necessary strength and support for long, rough hikes.

- Buy the best boots you can afford but have the child wear two pairs of heavy wool socks. As his feet grow, you can adjust wool and cotton socks to assure a snug and comfortable fit.

- Recreational Equipment, Incorporated, in Seattle, a climbing equipment cooperative, notes that many mountaineering stores allow trade-ins on good used boots. If you can find such a store, you can at least get something out of junior's outgrown footgear while you are fitting him for this year's treks.

- The old hand-me-down principle works with boots if you have family or friends who can cooperate. A variation on this theme is placing newspaper ads for exchanges with other families. In areas with a lot of recreational activity, you may be surprised at how many households have accumulations of outgrown boots.

Packs are probably the easiest hiking equipment formula to work out. The strongest member of the family is probably going to have to bear most of the load. That is the tent or tents, most of the cooking utensils, and most of the food as well as individual gear. This means a heavy-duty frame pack with a large capacity (say 4,500 cubic inches). The other adult can share some of the community gear such as pots and pans and some food as well as personal equipment. A small frame or load-bearing softpack should be sufficient.

Young children cannot be expected to carry much more than a token cargo. A top-opening daypack with a sleeping bag, toiletries and miscellaneous childhood necessities will probably be all the weight they can bear. Older children, ten to twelve, can wear a small frame pack and start to share their part of the burden, but it is probably wise to keep the bulk up and the weight down so that even though their packs look swollen, they are not going to be uncomfortable under the load.

Gauging the weight a child can carry and is going to be willing to carry, is a difficult problem. Some kids are surprisingly strong and cooperative while others take some coaxing and pampering. You can always start them out at the trailhead on the heavy side and absorb the excess weight among the adults later on up the trail.

The important thing to remember when planning family hikes and distributing the load is not to strain anybody. If a child or spouse is burdened or uncomfortable on the first outing, it is going to to be much more difficult to convince that person to try another.

JOINT PURCHASES

There are hundreds of parties hiking thousands of miles yearly who started hiking together and continue to hike together. On the other hand there are thousands of former parties that don't go anywhere because one or more of them discovered that there are better things to do than mingle with mother nature. The point is, unless you are really sure of the friendship and enthusiasm of your prospective hiking chums, it is probably unwise to jointly purchase community equipment.

The organization of parties should probably be built around specific hiking objectives. This does not mean that the same people are never going to hike together on a regular basis, but it does mean that it is difficult to know, when two or more people are just starting to hike, which of them will be going into the hills every weekend, which will be backpacking once or twice a year, and which will take up golf.

Each backpacker who is not ordinarily a family hiker should probably buy his own basic equipment. When a party of individuals is formed there will probably be duplication in available tents and stoves but it is easy to coordinate the packs and leave unnecessary equipment at home.

Having your own equipment leaves you with the freedom of packing it up and taking off on your own at any time the hills beckon. Solo hiking and solo mountain climbing are frowned upon in books and by most sensible people, and discouraged by many park officials, but there is a magic about being in the wilds by yourself that transcends good sense. However, that is another matter and something that every hiker should take up with himself after he has earned journeyman status.

CHAPTER THREE

Choosing and Procuring Equipment

Modern backpacking and mountaineering equipment is a genuine wonder of our technological age. It is one of the few areas of material development where substantive advances in design and function are achieved regularly without sacrificing the basic principles of the equipment or the traditional high quality of workmanship.

The manufacture and use of backpacking equipment does not deplete natural resource reserves or pollute the environment (although most clothing is made from petroleum-based fabrics). Workers, in general, are well-paid and well-treated and in many cases, are part-owners of the shops; most shops are locally owned and nobody gets extraordinarily rich from the sale of backpack gear. And the equipment itself not only doesn't maim or kill, it actually tends, because of its structural delicacy and light weight, to foster care and cleanliness in the wilds.

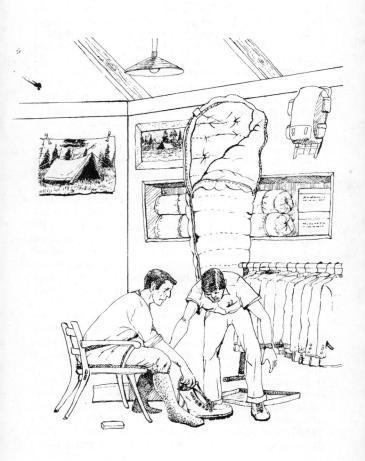

From the handful of outfitters and manufacturers that existed fifteen years ago, numerous small shops and stores have sprung up to meet the demands of an army of critical and quality-conscious hikers and mountaineers. There must be enough business to go around because all of the old established firms and most of the small shops continue to exist, but the competition remains incredibly sharp. Backpackers and mountaineers have traditionally been willing to try new ideas, and every year or so a new approach to one of the fundamental needs evolves. These new slants on old problems—such as dome tents and weight-bearing softpacks—quickly become accepted and go through a period of refinement and modification throughout the industry.

This unique emphasis on both technological advancement and traditional workmanship makes equipment buying an interesting and compelling (if expensive) sideline to backpacking. I know a number of people who spend as much time reading catalogs and shopping as they do hiking. Just about anybody who hikes and mountaineers a lot has more than one change of basic gear, and often closets full of obsolete equipment they no longer use.

Initial expense notwithstanding, if you and your family or friends decide that backpacking is better than Saturday night on the town and Sunday afternoon football, you should have your own equipment.

Shopping for, buying, and using your own gear is something you will eventually want to do. Renting gear might be a good idea for the first trip or two but the returns diminish rapidly, and after ten trips you could have paid for equipment of your own. Habitual borrowing can lead to strained friendships, especially if your schedule conflicts with that of your friends.

BOOTS

Boots are the one hiking essential that should be purchased. You can go second-class with mass-produced field or hunting boots, but you will more than pay the difference in blisters, sores, and uncomfortable feet.

Why? Because good hiking boots are specially designed and carefully made to perform specific functions. They have thick, lugged soles to prevent slipping and to insulate, acting also as shock absorbers to the bottoms of your feet from sharp rocks and the weight of your pack from the top. They have padded ankles which can be bound tightly to prevent twisting and straining. They have baffled or overlapped tongues to protect your feet from snow and water, and they are lined to absorb perspiration, and they keep your feet warm.

High quality boots are made of specially selected tanned and treated leather. The better manufacturers have their own processes, but good hiking boot leather in general is nearly waterproof, incredibly wear resistant (in more than fifteen years I have never actually worn out the leather of my trail boots), and stiff enough to absorb shocks and provide ankle support.

A good pair of backpacking boots weighs from $3^1/2$ to $4^1/2$ pounds, depending on the terrain you will be hiking and how durable you want them to be. There are lighter boots made by good makers but they are for hiking without a pack, and don't have the necessary sole and ankle support to hold up under

Styles of Boots
Top: Two-piece hinged. *Bottom:* One-piece with baffled tongue.

heavy loads. There are also heavier boots for mountaineering with very thick, inflexible soles which, when added to the extra weight, can really tire your feet.

Most good boots are imported from Italy, Switzerland, France, Austria, and Germany but there are several domestic firms making fine footwear. The problem in buying any good boot is getting a proper fit, and this is not as easy as it might seem. Foreign-made boots are normally longer for a given size than domestic ones. European boots are also much narrower than American feet on the average, offering only a narrow and skimpy medium size. Most American made boots and some imports now include honest medium and wide boot lasts in their lines, so that the problem now is to find a store having your length and width in stock.

You should shop for your boots at a reasonably equipped mountaineering and backpacking store. If you have to make a special trip of 100 miles to shop at a good mountaineering store for your boots, it may be worth it.

Mail order outfitters require a tracing of your stockinged feet; most of them offer returns or exchanges if the boot absolutely won't fit, but you are stuck with them if they seem to fit in the house but burned your feet on the trail.

The clerks in backpacking shops are generally hikers themselves and know what constitutes a good fit. The same can be said of mail order firms but they have less to work with in a foot tracing. In general, I have found backpacking shops extraordinarily conscientious, but if the clerk tries to sell you a number ten medium because they don't have a 10$^{1}/_{2}$ wide, you had better take all of your business elsewhere.

In fitting a boot remember two things: One of your feet is undoubtedly a tad larger than the other (usually the right), and both will be substantially larger on the trail than in the store. The stress, strain, and irritation of long hikes will swell your feet; how much they swell depends on the individual and the conditions.

My first hiking boots were reasonably good Italian affairs fit to my normal shoe size, which is eleven. I carefully broke them in with short jaunts around the hills, then loaded my pack and headed for Britain. I landed in the south of Scotland and intended to walk all the way to Inverness with my shiny new boots and fifty-pound pack. I got about fifteen miles out of Edinburgh before my feet were ready to defect. Somehow I made it but I had to make several two-day camps to allow my feet to deflate to the size of the boot. When I got to Aberdeen, on the way back down, I bought a new pair of size 11½ boots and threw the old ones away. Since then, I have increased my boot size to twelve and insist on boots that are of ample width.

The moral to the yarn, of course, is to be sure you compensate for expansion when fitting boots. You can run around the block a couple of times until your feet begin to swell, or you can wear two pairs of heavy wool socks and cram two fingers down the back of the boot before lacing. The two fingers and the socks should give you ample room to accommodate expansion and enough room to give your toes a buffer area before they hit the end of the boot.

If the boot feels comfortable unlaced, kick your heel back and string them up as hard as the traffic will bear. You will probably feel some pinching along the outside of the balls of your feet. This is alright because you want them to be snug, and adjusting these fine points of fit is the whole reason for breaking the boots in. But if the pinch on the ball is more than just a little annoying or makes you seek to relieve it by walking on the outside of the boots, you had better look into a wider pair. Good boots will give a little with wear but they are built to be tough and rigid so the process of expanding them a great deal can be long and painful.

If you can stand in the boots comfortably with the laces tightly drawn, you probably have found a match. But give them a good workout around the shop. Walk around, jump up and down on the balls of your feet. Find a stairway and ascend and descend a couple of times; does the heel get in your way going up? Do your toes touch the end of the boot on the way down? Keep them on and stay on your feet for fifteen or twenty minutes, as you look over other gear. If you don't feel more than minor pressure on any part of your feet, buy them.

But before you hand over the cash, check the boot carefully. There are a number of ways of assessing the general quality of a backpacking boot. Good boots are made to outlast the sole, which can be replaced. This means they always have a welt attaching the uppers to a midsole which represents a platform for the outsole. There are essentially three ways of attaching the midsole:

- The Goodyear welt is characterized by one row of stitches all around the sole of the boot. This is probably the most common method of constructing good boots, but not necessarily the strongest.

- The Norwegian welt adds another row of stitches to the upper sole connection and allows the bootmaker to lap the upper over the midsole for a sound, waterproof fit. The Norwegian system requires more material and is normally heavier than the Goodyear, but stronger.

- The lightest acceptable method is called the Littleway construction. Inside the boot and under the innersole you will see two rows of stitches holding the upper to the midsole. This method is probably not as strong as either of the other two but it is considerably lighter. Many bootmakers use all three of these methods on boots of different weight and function in their lines.

Inside of the boot you will notice fine, glove-leather lining. This lining conceals padding in the heel and should run all the way around the toe. In many cheaper boots, the lining either ends at the base of the tongue or is only glued to the toe lining. Insist on full lining, and stitching rather than glue at the connection.

The workmanship of the stitching throughout the boot is a general indication of overall quality. Pay attention also to the leather; it should be clean and hard, regardless of whether it is rough or smooth.

The choice between speed laces and plain boot eyes is largely personal. The big, shiny speed lacing hardware and hooks look impressive and make the process of getting the boot laced a little easier, but they won't hold any better or even as well as plain eyes, and they do add some weight.

Breaking-In and Care of Boots

There are a lot of formulas for quickly breaking in boots, such as taking a warm bath with them on or walking them up and down a stream, but these may

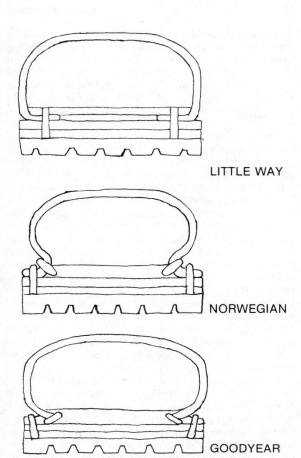

LITTLE WAY

NORWEGIAN

GOODYEAR

Boot Welt Construction Types
Top: Littleway (inside-stitched). *Middle:* Norwegian double-stitched. *Bottom:* Goodyear welt.

do more damage than good and part of the price of a
fine pair of boots is a little extra patience during
break-in. Before you wear them, treat them with a
silicone-based preservative. If, after wearing them
for several hours, you still feel an annoying pinch on
the sides of the ball, apply a little neatsfoot oil or oil-
based shoe preparation to the areas on either side.
Don't get any oil on the rear of the boot where it is
padded; oil will rot foam padding and ruin the
boots. There is also a mechanical way of removing
pressure: Adjust the laces around the pressure point
so that the areas above and below the painful spot
have doubled laces to relieve the tension in between.

After boots are broken in, they will still need
regular maintenance and care. Perhaps after every
long hike, or two or three short ones, you should go
over them well with silicone-based shoe preservative. If you think there is a good chance of getting
wet, or if you are planning a hike in snow, you will
want to seal the seams and treat the leather with a
snow-sealant. I use Goodyear Pliobond cement for
the welt and other exposed seams and Sno-Seal,
a wax-based waterproofing, for the leather. The
sealant and cement wear off after a long hike so you
should re-cement the seams first, then apply silicone
to the leather before applying another coat of waterproofing.

Shoe trees are good for keeping the uppers in form
and condition and to prevent warping in the leather
or composition midsole. If the midsole does warp, it
usually does so at a rate different from that of the
rubber outsole which results in separation of the
two, and the premature necessity of resoling. Shoe
trees cost about $5 new, but used ones are often
available in local thrift shops.

Another trick to keep shoe body and sole together

is adding brass screws or lumberman's studs to the outsole-midsole connection. If you use screws, make sure they are real brass (steel will corrode), and that they are not long enough to penetrate into the inside of the boot.

There is one more thing about hiking boots that should be noted before we move on. They are hiking boots and not casual or street shoes, even though you may need that dual purpose as a justification for buying them. The soles are too rigid and the uppers too stiff to be really comfortable on level surfaces and one mile of walking on concrete or paving will sand the expensive and essential lugs down farther than ten miles of the most rugged mountain trails.

SLEEPING BAGS

Now that you have a new pair of boots that cost you a bundle equivalent to a portable television set, and you can't even wear them on the streets to show them off, let's look into yet another esoteric and limited-utility piece of equipment.

You can get away with borrowing or renting sleeping bags but you will find, after a couple of trips, that crashing in somebody else's bag can lead to just enough insecurity to disturb your sleep. On the other hand, a well-chosen bag of your own is familiar, cozy, and homey enough to compensate for the hiking jitters.

Your first decision in shopping for a bag is going to be the kind of batting or filling used to produce the loft. The loft is the distance between the layers of a well-fluffed bag. It is the insulation that allows you to retain enough of your body-generated heat to keep yourself comfortably warm. The amount of loft you buy should be strictly governed by the night-

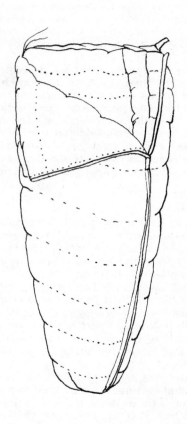

Semirectangular Sleeping Bag

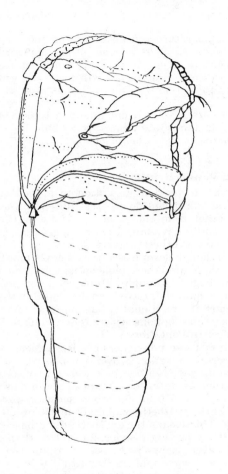

Mummy-Shape Bag

time temperature you anticipate on the coldest of
your hikes. About two inches of loft is regarded as
sufficient to keep most people warm at freezing
temperatures. Four inches will keep you warm to
about -50°F. (-45°C.), but will roast you at 50°F.
(10°C.).

Therefore, if you live and intend to do most of your
hiking in temperate climes, you would be wise to
aim for about two inches of loft.

Down Versus Synthetics

It used to be that insulation in a good quality
sleeping bag meant down—the fluffy, quill-less inner feather from eiders, geese, or ducks. Cheaper
bags usually have mixed feathers, grassy kapok or
stiff, heavy, synthetic batting.

Even though down is still the most popular filling
today, there are other viable options for good, lightweight bags. Two light, fluffy, and compressible
synthetic materials have been developed in the past
few years and most quality bag manufacturers offer
at least some options with either Celanese Polar-
Guard, or DuPont Fibrefill II.

Both of these newcomers are less expensive and
have certain advantages over down, as well as some
disadvantages. Neither produces nearly as much
insulation as down: one ounce of goose down will
insulate from 550 to 650 cubic inches of space. An
ounce of the synthetics will fill from 350 to 450 cubic
inches. This means the synthetic-filled bag will be
about forty percent heavier, for its loft, than down.
Down also compresses better than the synthetics and some makers claim that it holds up to
continuous squashing better than the synthetic fiber
materials.

Both fibers, however, are amazingly water-resistant. Both claim one percent water absorption which means the bag can be literally drenched and still provide warmth. It also means that these bags dry quickly after a soaking or washing. Down can remain soggy for days and loses all of its ability to insulate when wet. Neither synthetic drapes, or flows over the body quite as well as down but both of them provide better-compressed insulation on the bottom than down.

Price is perhaps the biggest benefit of the synthetics. An excellent quality PolarGuard bag costs about seventy-five to eighty percent of an equally good down bag by the same manufacturer. The goose down would be somewhat lighter (about three pounds compared to four pounds), but construction materials on both are about identical and represent a fixed weight.

There are, then, three primary considerations in making a choice between synthetics and down: price, stuffed size and weight, and the effect of water on the batting. If you live and plan to hike in an extremely wet climate, such as the Pacific Northwest, you might be better off with the fast-drying and warm-when-wet synthetics. On the other hand, if you intend to do a lot of really cold weather camping (sub-zero), down would be a better choice because it is lighter for the necessary loft. All other things being equal, the $25 or so saved on synthetic filling could be applied to other equipment.

The fine points of construction for down and synthetic bags differ slightly but quality and utility are universal. Cheaper versions of either filling hold the insulation between the layers of outer fabric by sewing directly through the top, the insulation, and the bottom. This method is much simpler but leaves insulation gaps at every stitch line and, consequently, cold spots in these areas. Better down and fiber bags eliminate these cold spots by either overlapping stitch lines or avoiding them entirely.

Better down bags normally separate the top of the fabric from the bottom by filling channels that run at right angles to the length of the bag with down. The most common method is slanted channel construction, followed by straight box and V-channels. All of these methods are acceptable, although there seem to be better arguments for slanted and V-channels, and the quality of the bag can almost be measured by the distance between each of these channels. Really good bags have narrow channels measuring six inches or less from the outside.

Another method of constructing down bags, and one that has been borrowed in better quality fiber bags, is the overlapping quilt. This requires positioning two sewn-through quilts together so that the loft of one covers the stitch line on the other. This method is cheaper and requires the extra weight of two additional layers of fabric but it does eliminate cold spots and results in a cozy and durable bag.

A common method currently used in many moderate quality fiber bags is called edge stabilization. The bat is simply left free, floating between the layers of outer and inner fabric, and the edges are tacked down at the ends and corners. This avoids the sewn-through seam problem when the bag is new but, with use and washing, the bat sometimes breaks loose from one or more points and leaves areas of the bag without any insulation.

The best and most expensive method of insulating fiber bags is called batting baffles. The method is a modification of the slant-tube construction in down bags and requires edge-stitching rectangular strips

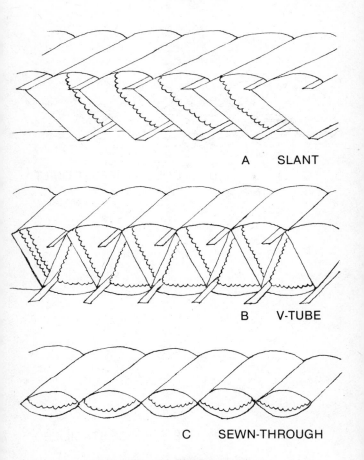

A   SLANT

B   V-TUBE

C   SEWN-THROUGH

Types of Sleeping Bag Construction
A. Slanted channel construction. *B.* V-channels. *C.* Sewn-through.

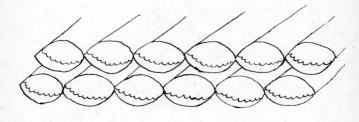

D   DOUBLE-OFFSET QUILT

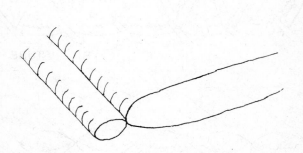

E   EDGE-STABILIZED

Types of Sleeping Bag Construction *(cont.)*
D. Overlapping quilt. *E*. Edge-stabilized.

of batting to the top and bottom fabrics at an angle. You will pay extra for bags fashioned in this manner but the batting will be even and will tend to stay put through use and washing.

Nearly all bags, both fiber and down, share one annoying constructional feature, which in time will ruin any of them. The stitch lines are generally exposed on the surface of both the outer and inner shell of fabric. This means that every time you turn over, your sharp toenails (or hard points on your clothing if you wear clothing to bed), are fraying and severing the stitches that hold the baffles. When the stitch line breaks, it opens the internal baffle and allows the filling to shift around and, usually, to lump up at the lowest point in the bag. One make, Sierra Designs, avoids this problem by tucking the baffle stitch line under a pinch of surface fabric. You might look for bags that don't show an open stitch line on the inner and outer fabric.

Down is especially sensitive to moisture, dirt, or greasy body grime and it must be kept dry and clean to perform efficiently. When you reach camp, it is essential to fluff the down fiber out by unstuffing the bag and allowing it to pucker up in the air. Before crawling in, fluff or shake the bag a few times gently to evenly distribute the filling.

After every trip, dry the bag for a few hours loose on a line, then store it loosely on a hanger. If you leave it stuffed for long periods of time, the down will stay compressed permanently and will lose some of its loft.

All down bags used to call for dry cleaning or hand washing and gentle air-drying. Currently many makers agree the down and internal baffling can withstand gentle machine-washing and low-temperature machine-drying. But don't take my word for it, follow the washing suggestions of the maker. If you can't find any with the bag, write the company for recommendations. One point about either hand washing or machine laundering down bags: Never pick up the bag by grabbing hold of an end; the enormous extra weight of the water will probably tear the internal baffling or stitching. Roll the bag or fold it into a tight ball at the bottom of the front-loading washing machine or wash tub and cradle it to either the dryer or out onto the lawn. If you intend to air dry the bag, you will be wise to unroll it on a flat surface and drain some of the water before hanging it from the line.

Synthetics are a little less demanding than down. A little grime and moisture won't make much difference in the fluff and a little sunshine will keep them smelling fresh for a long time. When it does come time to launder, synthetics are infinitely machine washable in a front-loader with a mild soap. Dry the same as down and don't be too rough on it while it is soggy (although the spin cycle will probably remove most of the moisture and added weight).

PADS

The bottom of your sleeping bag, even the synthetic fiber types, compresses so much with your weight that there is little or nothing between you and the cold ground. You will need some kind of foam pad (don't even think about air mattresses), to cushion your weight and provide the necessary insulation. There are essentially two kinds available today—thick, cozy-looking, open-cell, covered pads, and puny, hard-looking, closed-cell pads.

The open-cell pads are bulkier to carry, a tad more

comfortable, and generally more expensive. The closed-cell pads, such as the Ensolite, roll down into a neat little package, provide excellent insulation and cost only about $8.

BACKPACK

About now, with boots under one arm and sleeping bag under the other, you should start looking for

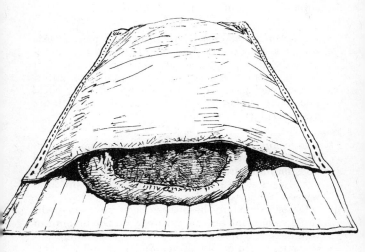

Bivouac Cover

Sleeping bag and pad go into this easy-to-make bivouac cover for sleeping out under the stars. Sew a breathing nylon top ample enough to cover your sleeping bag onto a waterproofed nylon bottom.

something to put them in. Backpacks are probably the most easily borrowed or rented of all your basic equipment, and it is even possible to save a lot of money with the cheaper packs, so long as you keep your load-weight down. If you do decide to buy one, you should know something about the three fundamental styles.

Softpacks. Bags with shoulder straps but no frames, are probably the most versatile and are available in the widest variety of styles. These range from a 1,000-cubic-inch teardrop daypack to a 4,000-cubic-inch weight-bearing expedition pack.

Internal frame sacks. This style, with more or less integral supports on the back of the pack, is available also in a wide variety of sizes and functions. It includes the famous (or infamous) triangular-framed rucksack, which has blistered many a back, and some rather interesting bendable aluminum and fiberglass variations.

External frame pack. Almost synonymous with backpacking, this is probably the most widely used and manufactured pack today. The frame and pack are always separate and attached either by pins and wires or fabric tubes.

Choosing among these three basic styles is predicated somewhat but not entirely, on the amount of weight that will be carried. Obviously, a young child carrying nothing but a sleeping bag and a toothbrush is not going to need more than a small softpack. Look for 1,000- to 1,500-cubic-inch capacity, top-opening softpacks that can double as school or bicycle bags. You can spend as little as $10 for such

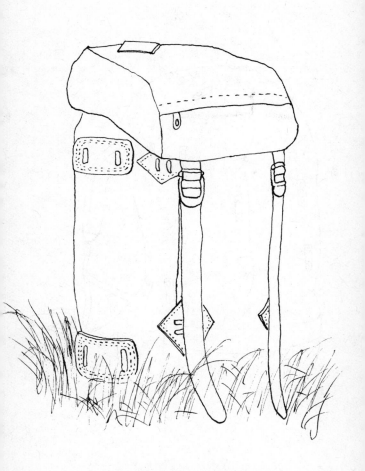

Soft Daypack Type of Softpack

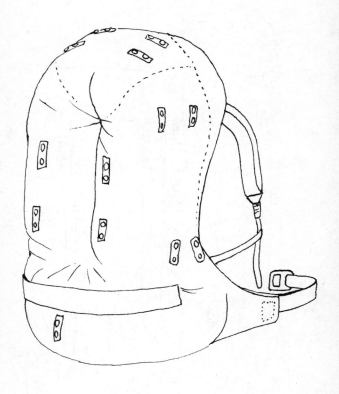

Weight-bearing, Self-Frame Softpack

Internal Frame Pack

External Frame Pack

a pack, but better-made and longer-lasting ones are now costing $20 to $25.

Small women and growing children who can carry their own equipment might look into large volume softpacks, which can carry twenty pounds comfortably, or one of the new generation of internal frame packs which can carry up to twenty-five or thirty pounds in a medium size. Many of these new packs have fiberglass inserts that wrap the pack all the way around your back and hips. They are quite comfortable and, in the better makes, very durable. Plan on spending from $30 to $50.

Full capacity packs, which can load up to forty-five or fifty pounds, are the most interesting because there has been more emphasis on development in this area. Frame packs are the most obvious choice. They are strong, dependable, and substantial and, indeed, are the best. The frame holds the loaded pack away from your back and distributes weight evenly between padded shoulder straps and a padded waist belt. There is usually room on the frame above and below the large pack to strap on additional gear.

The frame principle was perfected about twenty years ago by the Kelty Company and today scores of copies and modifications are available. Most people who head into the wilds with more than twenty-five pounds still use these frames. But there is an alternative.

During the last ten years a really incredible variation on the softpack has evolved, one that many veteran hikers and mountaineers feel will eventually supplant the primacy of the external frame. Mountaineers, especially, have always objected to the tendency of frames to catch on rocks and brush and throw the walker off balance. When

hiking along narrow ledges, this is not only annoying, it could be fatal. In the past, mountaineers used
frame packs to carry heavy loads to base camps but
changed to rucksacks or special summit packs for
the actual ascent under light loads.

Then, during the mid-sixties, a man named Don
Jensen began working on a revolutionary principle
in softpacks. He structured a virtually limp pack
into two vertical columns on top, buttressed by a
horizontal tube on the bottom. The bottom tube acts
as a weight-bearing waist belt and supports the two
rigidly stuffed columns up into the shoulder straps.
The result is a generic form of pack that not only distributes the weight over three points, (as a frame
pack), but actually suspends it over your entire hip
and back areas. The Jensen pack is currently being
made by the Rivendell Mountain Works but many
makers have modified the system into their own
lines. These packs are normally quite expensive,
costing from $40 up to $75, but you probably should
compare a loaded weight-bearing softpack against a
loaded frame pack before buying, especially if you
are considering any mountain climbing or mountain
hiking.

One advantage to the frame is its nearly universal
popularity. Almost every company that has anything to do with recreational equipment makes or
distributes a frame pack, and the stiff competition
seems to have resulted in a wide variation in prices.
You can buy an elegant looking frame pack, with
more pockets than you can count, from any discount
store for $20 to $30. They may not last more than a
season or two but they could make up for your recent
excesses in boots and sleeping bags. If you decide to
go first-class, you can spend up to $100 but $50 to

$70 will buy you a frame and a pack that will last many hard miles.

If you are going to spend that much on a frame, make sure it is soundly made. The tubing should be connected either with welds or stout fixtures. Cheaper frames are normally pinned or soldered together. The pack should be made out of relatively heavy nylon duck, at least eight-ounce, and probably should have a velvety smooth waterproof coating on both sides (although many good-quality packs are coated on only one side). The pack should be connected to the frame by a system of clevis pins and a spring wire to distribute the stress evenly.

The number of pockets and compartments offered in frame packs is almost infinite. Many veteran hikers are satisfied with one main body sack and maybe a flap pocket for maps and raingear. Many small pockets can make trail-handy things easier to find but they can be overdone. It is nice, however, to be able to isolate your stove and fuel from the rest of your gear in a side pocket (this goes for softpacks as well).

Several new compromises between the external frame and weight-bearing softpack provide another option in a large-capacity pack. These have integral frames and usually some columnar compartmentalization. Many have foam-padded backs and provide a stable platform for the pack weight.

Both heavily loaded softpacks and internal frame packs should be made of an extra strong synthetic weave such as Cordura nylon. Cordura is something like three times as abrasion-resistant as regular pack cloth and can stand up to the constant friction of rubbing on your belt, knife sheath, or passing rocks and trees.

Another thing you might look for, especially on soft and internal frame packs, are "cookies," or strap patches. A lot of things you can't get into your bag or don't want in it can be strapped to the outside with simple nylon-web buckle straps.

Good quality packs should last a long time without much fuss. It is possible to puncture or tear the fabric, in which case you should quickly stitch it shut (with your handy trailside sewing kit), and later patch the rent, and then waterproof the patch. Occasionally check the connections of the shoulder straps and belt for wear or pulled stitches. Zippers can go bad, and it is a good idea to carefully align the two edges before zipping up puckering sections or pockets.

SHELTER

The sleeping bag fits nicely in the bottom of your new pack and even the cumbersome boots only partially fill the remaining space; you may as well start looking for a shelter or tent to fill it out.

Shelter can be dirt cheap—even a $3 plastic tarp will do—but it won't do for long. You can expect about one pitching per tarp, so you may as well invest in a coated nylon fly tarp. It should be at least ten feet by ten feet (for one or two people), and will cost $25 to $40. But didn't we say you could buy a tent for $40? Indeed you can. Most discount stores will be happy to sell you one of their imported waterproof nylon "hiker's specials." There are many problems with these, poor workmanship and engineering notwithstanding. The main problem is the waterproof top. Ironically, while it is protecting you from the outside elements, the water barrier is subjecting you to an almost equally dampening inside element:

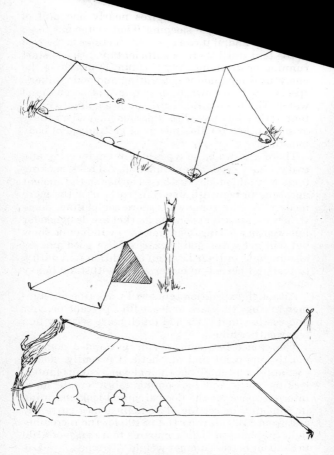

Different Ways of Pitching Fly Tarp as Shelter

                                    pint of
                                 ⌄r has to go
                              ⌐ngs to the roof
                           ⌐t quantity to start
                        ⌐s pint of drizzle to the
                     ⌐erating and your "hiker's
                  ⌐n in a quart of secondhand
              ⌐ line is: If you are going to buy a
           ⌐y one with a porous top and a rainfly
        ⌐er reliable means of getting rid of body
n.   ⌐e.

'⌐here are two basic types of tent engineering and
two primary types of tent function. All back-packing
tents available today are based either on the ancient
and time proven A-frame construction or the more
modern, and in some ways more compelling, dome
structure. Most tents on the market are designed for
fair-weather hiking, meaning they will handle snow
but will not withstand blizzards. Most good makers
also include in their lines an expedition tent with a
tunnel and beefed-up materials to withstand heavy
snow.

Although expedition tents will work fine for summer hiking, they are at least fifty percent heavier
and costlier and can't add much more security to a
fair-weather hike.

The choice between an A-frame and a dome is
mostly financial and aesthetic. Currently, domes
cost quite a bit more but their clever system of inter-
locking poles and blossoming fabric create more
internal space for the floor area and look charming
in a mountain setting. Two-man domes currently
cost from $160 (Jansport), to $190 for the incredibly
light Stephenson. This compares to a range of $100
to $120 for better summer weight A-frames.

Tents are the first piece of equipment we have dis-

Basic A-Frame Tent

Family-Size Dome Backpack Tent
This tent may be more economical and lighter than two or more smaller tents.

cussed that will be shared as a matter of routine and, as suggested earlier, you should plan carefully the use of tent space. Each person using a tent occupies a floor area of about fifteen square feet, or roughly seven feet by two feet. A two-person tent should be at least thirty square feet, three persons should have forty-five square feet and so on. Some two-person tents, with say thirty-five to forty square feet, have ample room for a medium-sized child but the child will preclude storing equipment. Also, the child will soon be big enough to constitute a full person so you might consider a regular three-man tent.

Larger tents are usually more economical in terms of per-person cost and weight. Gerry, a relatively old firm from Denver, for instance, makes three-season A-frame tents for two, three, and four persons. The two-person tent weighs seven pounds and costs about $140. This comes to $3\frac{1}{2}$ pounds per person and $70 each. The three-man version weighs 9.5 pounds and costs about $175, or 3.2 pounds per person and $58 each. The four-man tent weighs eleven pounds, or $2\frac{3}{4}$ pounds per person and costs about $210 or $52.50 per person. This amounts to enough of a bundle to justify planning your shelter needs around larger tents, provided you are relatively sure the extra space will be used on most trips.

There are several lines of less expensive tents, some of which are amazingly well made and engineered. Eureka, for instance, offers a large and popular line of tents one of which can sleep two people comfortably for six pounds of carrying weight and $75 to $90. They sell a four-man tent that costs only $115 to $125, weighs a mere 9.5 pounds and is actually roomier than many more expensive and heavier four-man tents.

Most better tents are made with a heavy coated nylon floor which should come up at least six inches of the lower sidewalls, and have uncoated light ripstop or taffeta nylon sidewalls or dome, and a coated ripstop or taffeta nylon fly. Most will provide everything you need for pitching, including poles and stakes, but it is wise to check inside the stuff sack to make sure it is all there. Most tents use jointed aluminum or alloy poles and better makers shock-cord the poles with elastic to facilitate assembly and reduce the possibility of losing a section. If your tent does not come with elastics, buy a shock cord kit and install it.

In general, the more you pay for a tent, the better designed it will be and the longer it will last. But there are a few things you should keep in mind and a simple maintenance ritual you should go through regularly. Start by pitching your tent as far as possible from a fire and preferably upwind of the blaze. Hot, airborne sparks can sear holes in your fly or canopy (or both). If you are stove-cooking inside the tent, make sure the fabric is flame retardant (most are by law), and you have an appropriate place to cook such as a floorless vestibule or cookhole. Light the stove outside the tent and leave the fuel bottle out. And, although a watched pot may take longer to boil, neither will it perform any surprise tricks; *never leave a lighted stove unattended.*

When you pitch, be mindful of stones, roots, sharp sticks, acorns, or pine cones that could puncture the waterproof bottom. I always take the added precaution of spreading a waterproof poncho under the tent, but that may be just a manifestation of my personal neuroses.

Pitching under trees has a number of disadvantages (which we will discuss later), but among them is the possibility of dead branches blowing or falling on the canopy.

There are also a number of do's in tent care. The waterproofed fabrics are extremely sensitive to the abrasion caused by dirt and miscellaneous jetsam. Sweep or shake out the floor area after every pitching and it is wise to wash off any dirt the bottom may have picked up from the ground. You might also sponge off the fly occasionally. After every trip you might take a look at the stress points, such as the stake loops, pole collars, and the shock-corded ends of the ridgeline, for wear and pulled stitching.

Another thing I do, which may not actually keep me any drier but probably helps me sleep nights, is regularly seam-seal the waterproof sewing lines. I use Pliobond but there are any number of good commercial sealants available.

Remember that sewing kit we talked about while buying a pack? Well, if you add a strip of self-adhering nylon repair tape you can field-repair any punctures, rips, or stressed seams in your tent as well as your sleeping bag, waterproofs, and down garments.

WATERPROOFS

You have probably just about cleaned your wallet and filled your new pack. The tent fits nicely next to the new boots (which you will be wearing on your feet while hiking), and while there is a little bit of money left and space available, you might as well look into a waterproof. For most hikers, and for most practical purposes, this means a poncho. Ponchos

Poncho, the Most Versatile Waterproof

are made of a sheet of rectangular waterproofed nylon with a turtleneck or hood hole cut in the middle for your head. Many ponchos today have extended backs to drape over your pack and they cover you nicely while still providing ventilation through the sides. They also double as ground cloths, quick shelters, and equipment covers in camp. Ponchos cost from $15 to $25 and considering their utility, they are a bargain.

A driving rain is about the only weather condition a poncho can't deal with as well as anything else available. When the sky starts coming down in sheets, most people are inclined to pack up and head for home. But often this isn't possible. About the only thing I know of that will keep you at least reasonably dry (if not happy), is a waterproofed knee-length pullover called a cagoule. A cagoule, along with knee-high gaiters or rainchaps, can maintain a constant dry clamminess while you are waiting out the storm. Cagoules cost from $30 to $40 while gaiters (which you should have anyway), run about $15 to $25. Rainchaps are cheaper than gaiters (about $7 to $10), but do not protect you nearly so well in the critical area of the feet and calves.

SEW-IT-YOURSELF KITS

One way of getting around at least some of this enormous expense is simply to make your gear yourself. All of the basics we just discussed, except boots, can be stitched together from kits by people with average talent at the sewing machine. Pre-cut and packaged sleeping bag, tent, waterproof, and back-pack kits cost from about two-thirds to three-quarters of the amount the finished products would

Wet-Weather Protection
Left: Gaiters. *Right:* Cagoule.

Sew It Yourself
Just follow the easy directions and . . .

cost. Several different firms either specialize or have sew-it-yourself sidelines and many can be found at your local fabric or sewing shop.

Whether you bought them readymade or stitched them up yourself, you now have most of the durable basics. Go home, count your gains and your losses, and get a good night's sleep. Because tomorrow we are going grocery shopping.

CHAPTER FOUR

Food and Cooking Necessities

For some peculiar reason, the culinary aspects have always demanded and received a disproportionate amount of exposure in camping and backpacking literature. Many nineteenth-century woodlore books contain an enormous amount of detail on how to sizzle tender victuals over painstakingly prepared coals in elaborate pits. Most recent backpacking books have at least several chapters on stove or hot-coal cooking and there is currently an immensely popular epicurean's guidebook to sumptuous trail-side cuisine.

And all this in spite of the almost universally acknowledged fact that anything, even the tongue out of your boot, tastes good after a hard day on the trail.

It is almost as if the writers of outing and backpacking books have felt compelled to attract their readers to the trails by dangling mouth-watering accounts of high mountain fare before their noses. And what quicker way to anybody's heart than through the stomach? But let's assume you are interested in taking off into the wilderness and living like a lean nomad for a couple of days. I am not going to tell you that the only way to make the trail tolerable is to haul along grandma's hand-me-down eight-pound Dutch oven or even the five-pound kitchen skillet. If I did, they might go up the first time but I would wager they wouldn't be included on the second trip.

Nor am I going to try to talk you into fresh fruits and vegetables or meats, or even canned goods. Fresh produce tends to go rank, stale, or mushy quickly and meat is normally well on its way to rotting long before you reach camp. Canned goods, even the varieties that were originally designed to be packed around like Spam, constitute (in the can and the liquid), a lot of extra carrying weight, and there is always the problem of disposing of the can after it is emptied. (Of course *nobody* ever leaves cans and containers on the trails or mountains; when they are finished with them, they carefully bend them up and store them in their sleeping bags for safe-keeping. Those mounds of fresh beer bottles, pudding tins, and chili cans you see all over the forest floor actually grow there.)

Seriously, though, everybody has good intentions of carrying their awkward garbage out (the trails to heaven are literally lined with good intentions), but one look at any trail will tell that most people don't do it. Canned goods are not worth the weight and trouble and should be left in the cupboard, where they belong.

FOOD

This staggering around through the hills under an enormous burden of extravagantly expensive equipment, presumably eating nothing but roots and berries, is probably starting to sound pretty tiresome. Although there are people who pride themselves on scavenging the simple fare nature leaves on the trails during the summer, there are whole varieties of packaged and dried foods you can pack that are light, clean, wholesome, and tasty. These include the common supermarket varieties of dehydrated packaged foods; the grains, cereals, nuts, and dried fruits available from organic health food stores; and an entirely new and often tantalizing generation of freeze-dried mountain foods.

For your first backpacking hike of one or two nights in the warm summer hills, you are not going to have to worry too much about maintaining a balanced diet. Most Americans could probably hike twenty miles in two days with no food at all and not feel any pain other than a healthy hollow in their stomachs. But you are not going up to pit your stomach against the wilderness or to prove anything, you are going hiking to have a wholesome, happy experience. And your exertion-sensitized appetite, satisfied over trail snacks and a tasty evening meal, is certainly part of this experience.

Fortunately, most tasty trail foods also have at least some nutritional value. The dietary elements most bodies need to keep functioning at a high level over the long haul are protein, carbohydrates, and fats. Most anything you buy off the supermarket shelf has bits and pieces of all of these, and practically all the prepared freeze-dried dinners are balanced meals.

The eating habits of veteran backpackers can be broken into two schools. There are those happy, leisurely folks who plan relatively relaxed hikes with plenty of time for long lunch breaks and comfortable evening camps around stoves or crackling campfires preparing and enjoying sumptuous meals. Then there are the adventurous and curious types who sacrifice long lunch and snack breaks for a side jaunt on the ridge to the left or a climb down to the lake below the trail. They normally end up pitching a camp at the last flicker of the gloaming and hurriedly fixing a carefully preplanned meal. There is no qualitative difference between the two, both would probably reach a given objective at about the same time (although the adventurer would probably see more territory along the way). One merely sacrifices the possibility of treading new ground for the sensual magic of quiet moments in the mountains while the other is willing to forego the serendipity of a mixed meal for the chance he may see something that nobody has ever seen before.

The method of packing food for each of the two schools normally marks their adherents. The adventurers know exactly what each meal on the trail will consist of and each is usually packaged separately so it can be selected from the kit and poured into a simple utensil quickly and in bad light. Adventurers are inclined toward the freeze-dried foods, which require only a sopping of hot water but many older and poorer adventurers still cling to old dry cereal mixtures and dehydrated dishes.

Those of the leisurely school also prepackage their meals but the packages are large and more diverse and there is usually a separate package of spices and garnishes and a little "something extra" for each evening's pot. Those who like to savor their meals and moods are also more inclined to carry greater variety of cookware, which we will examine in detail later.

Whichever class you eventually fall into, it is

probably wise to start out with tasty snacks and planned meals you can look forward to.

Freeze-dried, packaged meals and meal components are often incredibly good, although sometimes they taste more like texturized cardboard. They are remarkably light, with a carrying-to-eating weight ratio of about five to one (a ten-ounce package makes a fifty-ounce meal), and even more remarkably expensive. A beef stroganoff forty-eight-ounce dinner from one of the best producers costs about $4. The high cost is due to the initial cost of preparing the meal added to the expensive process of freeze-drying and packaging.

Freeze-dried dinners come in a large variety from several processors and might be, all things considered, your best bet for dinners on your shakedown hike. There are many brands to choose from. A party of four might want a cheese with ham dish and a side dish of peas one night for about $5, and a chili and macaroni dish with green beans the second night for about $4.50. If you have time, a liquid dish such as packaged soup should take out any growls that might remain and you could add a dessert of either instant pudding (which you can buy for 25¢ to 35¢ from your grocer, mix with instant milk, and cool in a nearby stream), or freeze-dried pudding which will cost about $1. Tea and instant cocoa are old-time favorites around the evening camp and prepare quickly and painlessly with boiling water and grocery-shelf packages.

You can also go freeze-dried for breakfast with omelets, cereal, or pancakes and syrup at about $1 per five-ounce serving. Or you can take along instant pancake batter, dried eggs, or instant oatmeal and sacrifice a little cooking and cleanup time. I really like the packaged instant oatmeal (especially the maple-and-brown-sugar-sweetened kind), which I mix with a little squeeze-tube-packaged peanut butter, a pinch of bran, and boiling water. This simple breakfast is quick, cheap, reasonably wholesome and has an added benefit which we will discuss in hushed tones later.

If you enjoy a morning cup of coffee, why not have some? You can easily store enough freeze-dried or instant coffee for eight to ten cups in a modest-sized plastic pill bottle. Sugar can go in another pill tube and instant milk out of a packaged envelope will add the accent.

Lunch on the trail for most veteran hikers is a series of short stops, starting an hour or so after breakfast and ending when your evening campsite objective is sighted on the next ridge. Most seasoned backpackers simply dig into a bag of evil-sounding but usually delicious "GORP" (Good Old Reliable Peanuts), whenever they get a bit hungry or tired. There are probably as many GORP recipes as there are hikers but most of them are either based on or include nuts of some kind. Nuts are an extremely efficient food, containing adequate supplies of at least three of the four nutritional necessities.

To a mixture of nuts, including cashews, roasted peanuts, and hazelnuts, I add a lot of granola cereal, raisins, and coated chocolate drops (the coating keeps the chocolate from melting and smearing all over fingers, pants, the GORP bag, and anything else it can fall or run onto). The combination of in-gredients makes these protracted lunches easily wholesome enough to keep you going until dinner with good nutritional building foods as well as ample quick-energy sugars. The strong emphasis on roughage and cereals also helps solve one of the most common and annoying problems of backpacking: constipation.

Most books will tell you in great detail how to construct and maintain a sanitary latrine but few of them give you any advice on how to get your body to use it. The combination of stresses on your system and eating habits on the trail is probably responsible for the normal inability to have regular bowel movements during overnight or two-day hikes. Many hikers I know don't even bother to carry toilet paper on short trips and merely reconcile the headache and stuffy feeling as a negative trade-off for the wilderness experience.

The grains, the breakfast oatmeal and bran, and the granola cereal in the GORP, tend to work their way through to the bottom of your digestive tract in a hurry. When the cereals have pushed everything in front of them to the rear, it can mean a sudden emergency stop on the trail. I usually carry, on the outside of my pack, a small mountaineer's trowel for such emergencies. As quickly as possible, I find a suitable spot where a foot-wide, foot-deep hole is not going to hurt anything (usually away from perennial vegetation and on as gentle a slope as possible). Afterwards, the hole should be filled up and nature will take care of the rest. I think one of the worst things you can do for your regularity is to attempt to compel your body to get it over with before breaking camp in the morning. This may work at home in time for you to catch the 9:15 but it is a different story on the trail. I think the urgency of the latrine staring at you from behind the bushes while everybody else is going about breaking camp actually tends to tighten up your system. Let it happen whenever and wherever it will and reconcile yourself to a short break in the hike.

Cereal-catalyzed excrement, which I fancy scours everything out of your stomach and intestines, is usually loose (sometimes alarmingly so), but I have found that whatever remains in the body is normal and healthy. Another slight drawback to the cereal scouring method of trail bowel-moving is the gas that sometimes accumulates. This can be disturbing to people behind and downwind of you but it usually doesn't last long and it is all for a good cause.

So much for digestion in all of its forms.

STOVES AND COOKINGWARE

The idyllic mountaineering scene usually consists of twilight over a grand vista broken in the foreground by wisps of smoke and several happy and hardy people sitting around a glowing campfire drinking tea and eating hardtack (or some equally romantic dish). Fires have always been a part of the common concept of the wilderness experience and at some times and some places, they still are, but in many areas of the country, including many of the national parks, fires are strictly forbidden. In many other areas, increased recreational use has made the practice of using campfires at least ecologically unsound. There are many wilderness travelers in the hills today who would no sooner build a campfire than burn their own home, and for much the same reason. The point is, if you do enough hiking in enough places, eventually you are going to have to carry some means of cooking food which for all practical purposes means a stove.

There are basically two types of single-burner

backpacking stoves on the market today: the liquid-fueled, self-contained units and the new pressurized cartridge modular types. In general, liquid-fueled stoves reached the epitome of development about twenty years ago and have remained basically the same since. One of the few exceptions is the Mountain Safety Research Model 9A which consists of a pump-generator mounted on a separate fuel bottle attached by a tube to a burner-regulator assembly. The MSR stove is slightly more expensive than most (about $40), but is safer, hotter and more reliable than other self-contained liquid-fuelers.

Some of the old liquid-fuelers still available are really works of art. The Optimus 00 is made of gleaming turned brass and you will probably want to put it on your mantel between trips. It is also an excellent pressurized alcohol burner and costs about $30. An extremely popular white gas burner is the Svea 123 which is also made of brass (although a bit less sophisticated in design), and self-generates an even flame in mild weather. It costs about $25. Another excellent and well-designed gas-burning stove is the Enders which is a bit more versatile although costlier (about $35), with its pressurized tank and feed. Self-generating stoves are less versatile than pumpers because they normally cannot maintain enough tank heat to keep up pressure during cold weather. All liquid-burners are at least somewhat fussy to light, and care should be taken to keep the generating parts clean and the fuel pure.

Pressurized cartridge stoves, on the other hand, are a snap to light and require virtually no care. The initial cost is also considerably lower but there are some drawbacks. A typical example is the Universal Sierra Stove which starts out costing under $20 sans cartridge. Cartridges cost $1.40 each and will burn

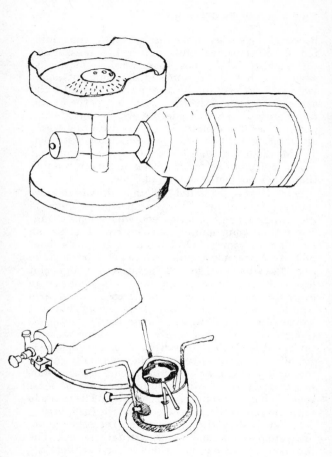

Backpacking Stoves
Top: Pressurized cartridge stove. *Bottom:* Mountain Safety
Research pump generator stove.

about three hours. The Universal will boil a cool
quart of water in about eight minutes (compared to
four minutes for the MSR stove), and folds neatly
into a lid-sized package for storage. But even though
the stove will fit nicely into any crevice in the pack,
the cartridges are bulky, beer-bottle-sized and two
should be carried, which totals a package much
larger than a liquid-burner and small fuel bottle.
And once again we have the disposal problem.
Empty cartridges have to be hauled out the same
way they were hauled in.

There are alternatives to stoves, such as Sterno
canned heat and army surplus heating tablets. Although both of these are much cheaper than stoves,
even on a long-term basis, they are also slower and
much more clumsy. The heat tablets are nice for
starting fires so you might pick up a few tubes (they
cost about 15¢ for six small pills or 30¢ for six large
wafers), and carry them in lieu of a stove on your
first few trips.

If and when you buy a liquid-fuel stove, you will
need a bottle for carrying extra fuel. Most fuels will
deteriorate plastic so look for either a cylindrical
aluminum bottle or a soldered tin affair in one-quart
size (which is more than ample for three or four
days).

So far as I know, no stove on the market today
comes with a nylon drawstring stuff sack, but all of
them should. When you get both your stove and your
cartridge or fuel bottle, buy or make a stuff sack that
will enclose both of them in a package to fit into one
of the outside pockets of your pack. This may require
piggybacking the bottle on top of the stove. Then get
two heavy-duty plastic bags and tightly wrap
both the stove and the bottle. Thus packaged, you
shouldn't have a problem with fuel or carbon de-

posits all over your pack. You might also add a
candle, a tube of heating tablets and a liquid-proof
package of extra matches to your "firebag."

COOKING UTENSILS

Now for a pot to put it all in. Many stoves have
custom cooking kits which are designed to rest comfortably on top of the stove when in use and nestle
together with the stove in the middle for storage.
This might appeal to you if you don't mind the faint
flavor of kerosene in your soup but I prefer to keep
my pots and stoves separate until it is dinnertime.
Also if you buy separate utensils, you can match
your needs much more accurately.

Discount stores, sporting goods shops and mountaineering shops veritably gleam with the polished
aluminum of different varieties of cooking kits
available. These range from $2.00 individual Boy
Scout type kits to a nesting pot for everything that
can cost up to $30. Before buying anything, you
should calculate your needs as accurately as possible. If you are hiking by yourself or with random
partners, you might be able to get by with some
variation on the Boy Scout kit which contains a one-
pint pot, a small frypan, dish, and plastic cup. Or, if
you like to shop around, there are some remarkably
fit veterans, including the celebrated GI canteen
and nesting cup which can keep your water cool on
the trail and boil enough for soups, tea or individual
freeze-dried dinners. Add to this one of the nicely
designed, flat-folding GI frypan-and-dish sets and
you can include fried and even baked dishes to your
cuisine. One of the niftiest surplus cook kits I know
of is an elegant French Army rectangular affair
(which fits comfortably in any pack), with a quart-

sized pot, a small rectangular frypan and a nesting plate. It is easily large enough for dinner for two and much better made than most commercial kits.

Regardless of which kind of kit or matched set you buy, make sure that everything in it fits into the largest pot, to reduce the total volume necessary for packing. This may exclude a large frypan so if you are especially fond of fried foods hang one of the new Teflon-coated pans on the back of your pack. A lot of people are uneasy about health aspects of Teflon, but it surely makes getting foods out of the pan and cleaning it considerably easier.

Naturally, each person should carry his own cup. If you are packing a GI canteen, the nesting cup will do fine. Otherwise, a stainless steel "Sierra" cup is light, easy to stash on your belt or in your pack and won't singe your lips with hot liquid. Each person should carry his own spoon and knife as well. The spoon can be a common table-variety stainless steel soup spoon with the back of the handle bent down into a hook. A soup spoon is large enough for stirring and the hook can be looped around your little finger while you are messing around with the pot. Your pocket- or belt-knife will easily do for any dinnertime functions. You can buy attractive knife–spoon–and–fork kits which comfortably nestle together in plastic pouches. Mostly everybody starts off by buying one of these sets, but usually ends up carrying just the spoon because the knife is redundant and the fork is superfluous.

As with stoves, pots seldom come in bags but most certainly should have one. Again, buy or make a nylon drawstring sack that fits over your nestled set. If you don't mind black, oily streaks over everything in your pack, you needn't bother.

The heavy, grimy soot that coats and clings to the

bottom of all your cooking utensils is probably one of
the toughest substances known to man. Fuel stoves
tend to anodize the bottoms of your pots and pans
with a thin but stubborn charry coat. And fires,
especially pine fires, bake on a thick, grimy coat of
tar which requires extraordinary heroism to scrape
off, so why bother?

The coloring actually won't offend anybody up in
the hills, doesn't add measurably to the weight and
actually helps absorb and evenly distribute heat for
quicker, more consistent cooking. Most veterans feel
there are better things to do in the hills than scour
cookware all day, and usually leave the soot alone
until at least the end of the season.

The insides, of course, are another matter
and should be thoroughly cleaned and scoured immediately after every use. The same bacteria that
can turn your stomach inside out at home can ruin a
hike and possibly endanger your life in the wilderness. Biodegradable soap, such as green medical
soap or Cutter's soap will do the job and won't hurt
anything in the hills as long as you are careful how
you use it. You can buy green soap in four-ounce
plastic bottles, that pack nicely and are ample for a
couple of days' cleanup chores.

Some campers carry along a separate vinyl dish-
pan but most merely heat some water until it is
marginally comfortable, pour it and a couple of
drops of soap into the dirty ware and scour carefully.
Afterwards, dispose of the water in a foot-deep hole
(never in or near lakes or streams) and examine the
insides of cookware for spots or discolorations.

Although green soap breaks up quickly in the environment, it can have an immediate and disastrous
effect on the physical and chemical composition of
living water.

Brass-screen scouring balls are fine except they are a bit bulky and tend to sop up grease and grime. I use the new nylon sanding pads which are little thicker than paper, can be formed around any corner or crevice in your pot, and wear forever. I usually keep one of these and a bottle of green soap in the bottom of my pot bag.

You will also need containers for water, at least a canteen for the trail and perhaps something for hauling and storing camp water. The double-wall, 1½-gallon plastic bags are really nice for camp water. Set on a flat surface, the lidded tap can be used like a spigot by putting pressure on the end of the bag; they fold up to practically nothing when not in use. If you aren't going to go the GI canteen route, pack your trail water in one of the many pint or quart crushable vinyl flasks or canteens available. Many hikers carry two small canteens—one with the remainder of last night's tea or a mixed fruit drink such as Tang, the other for plain old water.

VITAMINS

Although a carefully selected camp menu will probably satisfy most of the basic nutritional requirements, this thin, packaged fare can lead to deficiencies in some vitamins over the long pull. If you are a believer in vitamin C, bring along enough to keep you happy for the duration of your trip. Most mountaineers also take along specially formulated multiple-vitamin supplements generically called stress tablets. They are available in some form at most drugstores or mountaineering shops and are probably worth taking along.

CHAPTER FIVE

Add-ons and Debatables

The basics—those things you will need on the trail and probably have to buy for that purpose—have now been pretty well covered. They will take up most of the room in your backpack but there is probably still an empty layer in the top, a vacant corner here and a hollow pocket there begging to be filled. Good, because you still need a few more things, but don't panic because most of the balance of your pack can be easily scavenged from the house or your fishing gear.

NECESSARY EXTRAS

In the first place you are going to need clothes, in addition to those you start out wearing. If you are hiking in the mountains, you are going to find that even July mornings and evenings can be brisk. A thin wool sweater will help take the edge off the freshening air and you might even consider a light down jacket or shirt. At the same time a mountain night can be uncomfortably cool, the afternoon can be insufferably warm. You might want to add a light sunhat and a pair of walking shorts. You will also need a change of clothing including pants, shirt or sweater, underwear, and socks.

Socks are the one piece of equipment you will need in quantity. Some people with extremely sweaty feet will want to change often, maybe every two or three hours, rinsing (without soap) the worn pair in a stream and hanging them on the back of their packs to dry. In this case you will probably need at least two extra pairs of outer wool socks and two extra pairs of light nylon or silk inner socks (one set on, one set packed and dry, and one set drying at all times). The purpose of light-and-heavy sock combinations is to sufficiently insulate your feet from the inside of the boot and allow moisture to "wick" out of the light, inner sock onto the heavy outer sock. This reduces clamminess and friction, and keeps your feet clean and comfortable and should help to eliminate blisters.

If anybody in the party begins to develop an irritation or a blister, the hike should stop immediately and the sore area should be washed and treated with moleskins or blister pads (which ought to be in every first-aid kit). Uncared-for blisters have ruined many hikes, not only for the owners of the sore feet but also for the rest of the party who must slow down to the limping pace.

If you are starting out on your trip in the cool of the morning, wear clothing that can be stripped off in layers to meet the changing conditions of the day. Start off with, say, a pair of cotton pants (dungarees or regular walking pants), with a pair of athletic trunks underneath. A fishnet undershirt (with cotton panels around the shoulders), is a good basic garment that can help keep you cool in the heat and warm in the cold. Over that try a sweatshirt and, if it is cold enough, either a wool shirt or sweater on top. Remember that as you walk uphill you will be generating much more heat than you would standing and you should pre-compensate your clothing thickness to help reduce heat and sweating. Sweating is the body's natural but inconvenient reaction to excessive heat. It tends to sog up especially the upper garments and, in the case of cotton or down, completely eliminate any insulation value they may have when it does get cold. Your wet, clammy shirts can also cool your body too quickly through convection which can be extremely dangerous under some conditions. Even moderately cool summer evenings can lead to a deadly condition known as hypothermia, which will be discussed later.

In the spring or fall, especially if there is a chance of getting wet, you should probably supplant cotton clothing with wool. Dense wool such as whipcords or Malones offers better insulation when dry and remains warm even when wet. Knickers—knee-length trousers—are really nice because you can create ventilation by pulling down long socks and opening the hem at the knee while retaining the critical insulation over your thighs and stomach. Keep the fishnet undershirt as a foundation but you might replace the sweatshirt in cooler seasons with a button-front wool shirt.

You can buy a pair of Woolrich Mills knickers for about $35, or engineer a pair yourself by exhuming an old pair of wool pants from the cedar chest and cutting them off below the knee and add a simple hemmed-in drawcord closure.

Knickers

Homemade Knickers

Cut a pair of old wool dress pants below the knee and hem in a drawcord.

Cooler weather backpacking, especially in the mountains, usually calls for something a little cozier than a sweater. A down or synthetic-insulated jacket can be immensely welcome when the evening temperatures plummet below 40°F (4°C)—which can happen at any time in the high mountains—or as a buffer against a fresh morning after crawling out of the sleeping bag. Light jackets make dandy pillows too, stuffed loosely in a sleeping bag sack or into a wool sweater (which eliminates that cold-clammy nylon sensation against your face).

Jacket or Vest?

The same positive-negative trade-offs that applied to down sleeping bags should govern your choice of a lightweight jacket. Down jackets are lighter—and many feel sensually cozier—and they stuff down to practically nothing. On the other hand, the synthetic fills—Fibrefill II or PolarGuard—are cheaper, easier to care for, dry easily and quickly, and retain much of their loft and insulation when wet. The ability of these two synthetics to keep you warm, even after a drenching, is probably more critical in jackets than in sleeping bags because while a sleeping bag is normally protected either in your pack or tent, jackets are always exposed to the elements when in use.

Vests are another increasingly popular way of retaining body warmth. By eliminating the sleeves, they are cheaper and lighter and many people argue they will keep you equally warm and are better suited for hiking because they ventilate better during exertion. Frankly, I feel vests do not provide the necessary warmth full-sleeved jackets will for the same reason—they ventilate better; a lot of heat as well as moisture escapes through the open armholes.

Synthetics will save you about twenty percent in either vests or jackets. The Snow Lion Yosemite vest insulated with PolarGuard, for instance, costs about $5 less compared to the same vest insulated with down. Also, a jacket will cost about $10 or $12 more for either down or synthetic.

A stitch in time can save money, and jackets and vests are considered fairly easy sew-it-yourself kits to start with. A reasonably priced down vest kit is available from Frostline, and a down sweater kit, also sensibly priced, from Holubar is available for adults or for children.

Hats

Hats are a usually neglected but extremely important part of the wardrobe of a well-dressed backpacker. Their weight is negative in relation to comfort and they could actually keep you out of a lot of trouble in the hills. A white-brimmed tennis cap is ideal for summer hiking. It will shelter your head and face from the sun and allow your scalp to ventilate at an even rate. Conversely, a wool stocking-cap will save as much as fifty percent of your body heat during the chilly evenings and while you are asleep. Together, they weigh about half a pound (at most), and since you are always wearing one, you need only carry a couple of ounces in a fist-sized niche in your pack. There is an old mountaineering saying that if your feet get cold, put on your (wool) hat. And you might try donning your tennis hat if your feet get warm. So far as body heat control is concerned, you may be better off without your pants than your hat.

Gloves

Gloves may seem as out of place in summer hiking as a wool stocking-cap, but you are going to be surprised how often you wish you had a pair if you don't carry them along. Mountain evening temperatures in July can numb the fingers and so can a hot pot-handle. I would never even leave on a backpack hike without a pair of dainty GI wool fingerless palm socks and I often include one beat-up leather glove as a pot handler. If you can't find a pair of the GI gloves, you can cut the worn-out bottoms off a pair of wool socks and open a thumb hole in the side. They may be a little sloppy but they can keep your tucked-in fingers surprisingly warm.

Bandanna

The red bandanna commonly portrayed around the neck of cowboys and mountaineers was not worn for show, it is a highly useful tool in the wilderness. In addition to its common nasal function, a ban-danna can be used for quick bandages and tour-niquets, head-sweatbands, potholders (if you forgot your leather glove), trail markers, a friction insulator when using a rope and, indeed, around your neck to protect you from the sun. I usually carry at least one spare for every day on the trail or, during longer trips, three so that one can be in use, one clean and stored, and one drying after a streamside wash, at all times.

Extra Clothing

Extra clothing, buried deep in your pack in a watertight package, should be seasonally adjusted to cover the coldest weather you anticipate on your

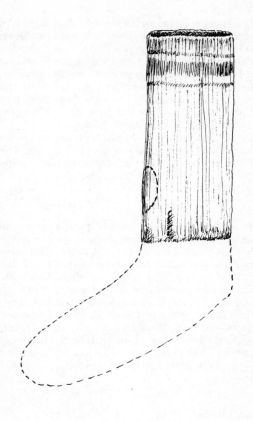

Palm Sock

Cut the top off a worn-out wool sock, slit a thumb hole, and stitch in a finger loop.

hike. This means that even if you start the hike in shorts or cotton pants, your spare pants should be light wool knickers to change into if you need something warmer. Your spare shirt should be wool, even if it duplicates the wool shirt you stripped off after the hike started. And don't forget a change of underwear.

Sundry Essentials

Although there are probably any number of things you will want on your first shakedown hike, there are only a few more things you will actually need.

A good, keen pocketknife is certainly one of the handiest things to be used on the trail. Its uses are too obvious and numerous to even mention, and if

Lock-Blade Folding Knife

ever you find yourself up in the hills without a knife, regretfully you will count the occasions you *could* have used one. Everyone in the party should have his own knife.

Any old pocketknife will probably do, for your first trip, but there are a number of knives available on the market that will do better.

The most commonly seen knife in the wilderness is the famous Swiss Army model. The genuine Wenger comes in sizes and blade functions (twenty-eight, to be exact), from a thin, two-blade to a bulging, sixteen-tool model that can hardly be called a pocketknife. You can buy a knife with a magnifying glass, saw, toothpick, and scissors (as well as nine other blades), for around $30 if you want, or a model with just enough blades to cover your basic needs at a considerably lower price. They are made of good edge-holding stainless steel that will hold up to almost any abuse except loss. There are any number of other Swiss Army type knives available, some Swiss- and German- made being quite similar to the Wenger in both quality and price.

The only tool on a pocketknife that is absolutely indispensable is the cutting blade. Although many veteran hikers would feel naked without their bristling Swiss Army knife, many others are going into the single-lock-blade belt knives. The lock makes heavy use of the cutting blade a lot safer because it can't close on your hand if the knife should happen to twist the wrong way.

You can pay a fortune for a lock-blade but there are many moderately priced and equally good knives on the market and several inexpensive but surprisingly good models. An example of a moderately priced knife with a lock-blade would be either the Gerber or Buck three-inch single-blade.

However, some remarkably good 440-c (extremely hard and edge-holding), stainless knives are offered by Precise, G-66, and Edge-Mark for about half the price. These knives are imported but come in a large variety of blade-size and style options and are adequately well made.

Your hunting sheath knife will do as a hiker's knife but you will find that the bulky belt holster tends to be in the way of your pack belt, and a bind on your hip.

Ropes

More rope is one of the things you normally wish you had when you are getting up to, or coming down from, anyplace on the trail. If you are backpacking in the mountains, especially the Rockies, you ought to have a good length of rope (about 100 feet), that is strong enough to support your weight on a fairly steep slope. It is understood that you are not planning any technical rock work or mountain climbing on your first trip, but many mountain trails are punctuated by small rock faces that are creampuffs when dry but slippery and treacherous after a rain. A reasonably stout rope can make getting up or down wet slopes much less of an ordeal. You don't need a big, heavy mountaineering rope but a quarter-inch, 1,600-pound strength, braided nylon rope doesn't add much weight (maybe a pound), costs about $6 and adds a lot of security to a tight spot.

No matter where you are hiking, you should carry a fifty-foot coil or two of one-sixteenth-inch braided nylon for supporting shelters, tents, making clothesline or light emergency use. A couple of fifty-foot lengths would be several dollars well spent.

Compass and First Aid

You will need compasses, preferably one for each member of the party, and every member should have a well-balanced first-aid kit. We will talk about both of these essential items in detail later on.

Matches

There are a lot of ways of lighting fires with the materials at hand in the wilderness, and most of them really work with time and practice. But none of them work nearly as well as a book of matches, so save yourself a lot of time and grief and carry plenty. I smoke a pipe and carry a supply of plastic-bag-waterproofed book matches in my pocket. I also carry at least two stashes of them in different parts of my pack, and in addition, I carry two small plastic-protected boxes of commercially treated waterproof safety matches in my emergency kit, along with my extra supply of foil-wrapped, freeze-dried grub.

Emergency Kit

This kit, which I call the burden of my anxiety, is always stashed in the bottom of my pack even though in sixteen years and thousands of foot-miles, I have never had the occasion to use it. It contains, in addition to a full day's fare and matches, two days' worth of vitamins and a tiny metalized plastic Thermos Space Emergency Blanket. The whole kit is tightly taped in a heavy plastic bag, which in turn, slips into a custom-sized, nylon drawstring bag. It weighs about a pound and takes up less room than my folded poncho. I am sure I never notice the weight and I really feel more secure knowing it is there.

Sunglasses

Sunglasses, another of those peculiar things like hats, that seem out of place in the wilderness and often get left behind, are a critical part of your equipment, especially if you are going to encounter snow. The dazzling reflection of a bright sun off snow, or even naked rock, can painfully irritate your eyes and may cause temporary blindness. If you are going to be hiking in a lot of snow, you might consider either special mountain-climbing goggles or ski goggles. These help cut down the peripheral glare as well as the direct blaze. Most of the time, however, plain drugstore glasses and clip-ons will do. I prefer Polaroid brand because, even though they are a bit more expensive than most other polarized plastic glasses, they definitely hold up and resist scratches much better.

Sunburn Cream

Another danger of sun in the mountains is sunburn. Even though the air is generally cooler up in the hills than it is in the lowlands, the rays of the sun are much more intense. People with good lowland tans can sizzle in the mountains. Most any good suntan cream will help and while you are at it, you might as well throw in a tube of lip wax.

Mosquito Dope

Depending on where and when you hike, you might need some mosquito repellent. I now do al-

most all of my hiking in the Rocky Mountain ranges
where cool nighttime temperatures tend to make annoying bugs diurnal. During the day when they are
about, I normally deal with them with a stiff upper
lip (which often gets bitten), or an acrid pipeful of
smoke. Mosquito bites don't bother me that much
and I would rather sustain a few than walk around
for several days with diverse layers of concoctions on
my body, inviting possible allergic reactions.

But I can remember harrowing nights in the
Adirondacks where fleets of various bugs assailed
me from all directions, and days in the marshes of
Michigan's upper peninsula where the swarms of
mosquitoes were so thick you could hardly see to
swat them.

If your hikes take you into biting-bug country, go
well-armed. There are several good preparations on
the market but not all of them will repel blackflies
and gnats. Consult locally about the nature of
resident bugs and favorite dope preparations.

Flashlight

Almost every book written on camping and backpacking since the invention of the flashlight has
recommended carrying one and I wouldn't want to
foster any new heresies so you might as well see if
you can cram one into your now bulging pack. I must
say, however, that I have never carried one and have
never regretted it. I know my equipment well
enough so that I can, and have, pitched my camp in
the dark. And I have my candle in case I feel restless
in the middle of the night. With regard to emergencies, I don't think any battery in the world will
last long enough to get you out of the hills at night,
and you are probably better off staying put. I also

don't believe that flashlights intimidate large animals such as bears, and again, you are probably better off with a low, quiet profile.

Toilet Tissue

There is one more thing you absolutely can't live without in that last vacant space in the pack: toilet paper. There are people who don't carry toilet paper, either because they are going to be too constipated to need it or because they feel that by using nature's own they will get some kind of transcendental revelation. But the message could get rather serious in poison ivy country. Toilet paper is neither heavy nor ecologically unsound (although it should be carefully buried and ought to be the largest trinket of civilization you leave behind).

ELECTIVES

Your pack is probably already about as full as you are going to want it to be, and that is alright because you should have just about everything you will need. But just about everybody takes along a few non-essentials, some large and some small, to make the trip more memorable. Just about every party in the hills these days has at least one camera. There is a lot to photograph up there and your friends or family always seem to show different sides worth recording.

Any camera will do if the pictures satisfy you, but there are several miniatures that pack easily and take excellent pictures. I don't like negatives smaller than thirty-five millimeters and for that reason I use a cigarette-pack-size Rollei C-35. The Rollei has a built-in exposure meter but no range-finder (which I often miss), and there are several

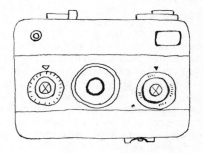

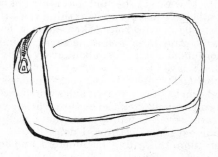

Compact 35mm Camera

other makes about the same size that have a range-finder and meter as well. The new sub-miniature, 110-cartridge-film cameras are really easy to pack and use, and take remarkably good snaps. They are also relatively less costly, the Kodak model costing only about thirty-five to forty percent of the cost of compact thirty-fives.

Cameras require a little extra care because of their sensitivity to water. You can easily make a nifty little bag out of waterproofed nylon with a pullstring bottom and a hole for the camera loop or straps in the top.

There is a lot of lore in each backpacking trip that can't be captured on film. It may be equally difficult to record the moods, momentary miseries and ecstasies of a hike in words but most backpackers try. I carry a small art tablet and a ballpoint pen to keep a record of landmarks, views, weather conditions, hiking times, bearings, and animals and plants, as well as word-worthy subject matters. I keep one book for each year and am building a small library to which I often refer for a pleasant memory or to help plan another trip into the same area.

The pad and pen go into a little waterproof nylon bag along with a paperback book (nothing too heavy in matter or material), for restless nights or lazy days.

Binoculars or a small, single optic lens can bring a lot of things you want to see or identify, up closer. One fall morning I was lounging in my sleeping bag on a saddle ridge between two of the highest peaks in Western Montana's Mission Mountain range. I was watching the rising sun slowly creep along the mountain to the southeast, spreading as it went, a hoary glow along the rock profile. Suddenly the glow exploded into a dazzling eruption of light, as if the still hidden sun were being amplified by a prism. Enchanted, I reached above my head and pulled out a pair of small-roof prism binoculars and focused in on a billy mountain goat, ashimmer with light as he stood on the summit of the mountain. We watched each other for about fifteen minutes until he got bored and moved out of sight. Those fifteen minutes more than justified the expense and bother of carrying the binoculars for me.

My glasses were Swift Trilyte eight-power roof prism binoculars which fold smaller than a pack of cigarettes, weigh 6.5 ounces and cost about $120. L. L. Bean sells an ultra-light roof prism eight-power monocular (one tube), for about $40, which weighs only two and three-quarters ounces.

Heavy hiking boots can become a bit confining around camp and most hikers hitch a pair of light-weight jogging or tennis shoes to the outside of their packs. The extra shoes are nice for loafing and light exploring, for fording creeks too deep for your boots, and for fishing.

Most hikes seem to end at remote lakes or streams and most hikers avail themselves of silly wilderness trout or other fish for a fresh main course for dinner. There are any number of backpacking fly and spinning rods on the market that break down into small packages but the cheaper ones are clumsy to use and the better ones are fairly expensive. However, you can sneak your favorite two-piece rod up with you by using the aluminum rod tube as a walking stick. Put felt, foam, or wadded paper bumpers on the inside bottom of the case and on the inside top so the bagged rod will fit snugly, then wrap the outside bottom with a couple of layers of masking tape and the upper six inches of the tube with a handle of cloth adhesive tape or leather. You might add a nylon sling around the top and bottom so you can carry it over your shoulder if you need both hands free.

Your reel should be the lightest you have, and don't be too extravagant with lures or flies. Wilderness fish are usually pretty innocent and two or three different spinners or a dozen assorted bright flies will usually make "a dinner make."

Don't overdo the bringing-in-the-bacon routine. Remember, upland lakes and streams have a much shorter growing season than your accustomed fishing waters and it takes fish a long time to reach maturity. The fish are usually overly hungry and it is no great honor to catch many more than you can use and leave the water sadly depleted or even barren. Keep only what you need for the next meal. In bear country this is almost a rule of survival because fragrant fish hanging from a tree are an open invitation to any bruin in the neighborhood, and they will often take more tithe than just the fish.

The final electives are a trowel and a towel. The trowel, which weighs only about two ounces, and packs easily anywhere on the outside of your pack, might almost be an essential. It is most useful for pushing out rocks and roots from your tent site, holes for dishwater, organic garbage and latrines, and tidying up the kitchen or fireplace. And they cost under a dollar at any backpacking shop.

Towels are also marginally essential. Many veteran mountaineers and hikers wouldn't go into the hills without one; an equal number of tempered hikers seldom bother with them. Use your own judgment.

FLUFF

And then there are the non-essential take-alongs which are pure fluff. These differ from electives in that their trouble and weight are practically never compensated for in use and comfort. This doesn't mean you won't see many hikers staggering under the burden of these superfluities, but you don't have to be one of them. These "security blankets" include blankets, pillows, folding seats, baggie toilets, gas lanterns, guns (which are illegal in most areas), portable radios and just about anything else including dinner ties and tails.

One of the nicest things about getting into backpacking is the perspective it offers on the difference between need and opulence. In our domestic lives, just about anybody can sell us just about anything because we have no measurable criteria for determining its real value. Consequently, our homes, cars, offices, and shops are littered with the useless along with the useful and the only way we can tell the difference is by measuring the amount of dust they accumulate.

But you are intimately aware of everything you carry on the trail. Your pockets bulge with the friendly familiarity of knife and compass. The things you carry in your pack to help support you in the wilderness are in turn supported by you through the long, hard miles on the trail. Anything that isn't necessary or at least measurably useful soon becomes a burden. The balance evolves into a tight, efficient toolkit with which you share a kind of symbiotic relationship: it depends on you to get into the hills, you depend on it to keep you safe and comfortable while there.

CHAPTER SIX

Health and Health Problems

There is a real, almost palpable metaphysical difference between the "real world" where we live and the "fantasy world" where we hike. Backpacking into the wilderness is almost like leaving the comfortable security of ordered and orderly civilization and walking off into the universe. We are leaving what we know exists for something that was, should be, or will be. In doing so we cut a lot of umbilical cords: telephone, roads, television, radio and that most secure line of all, the feeling that somebody is always nearby in times of need.

In the wilderness you are effectively on your own, relying on your own knowledge and resourcefulness and the experience and resources of your party. You are sacrificing two thousand years of civilized know-how and technology for these few flimsy barriers between you and potential disaster.

If anything happens to you or any member of your party in the wilderness, it happens quickly and furiously. A sprained ankle or appendicitis up here can kill you but at home they would most likely only inconvenience you for a few days. A casual dunking or a chill that might lead to a cold down below could result in life-sapping exposure when in the wilderness.

And if you are going up to avoid the mindful and mindless violence of civilization, you are going to find a certain amount of nature's orderly violence in the wilderness. Every step on the trail conceals a loose boulder or slippery foothold. Animals in the wilderness live by their own laws and you could violate one innocently but still have to pay the penalty. And the weather, especially in the high mountains, can change treacherously without reason or warning. Neither is there a phone on the tree, a ranger behind the bush, or a warm shelter over the next ridge. You and the equipment you brought with you are on your own.

These are things you should think carefully about before going up on your first hike. Some people will wisely realize that they cannot tolerate quite that much isolation and stay home or enjoy more secure forms of recreation. Those who want to go will learn what kind of problems they can expect from the wilderness—both generally and specifically in the area they intend to hike—and know how to either avoid problems or deal with them if they should occur. The only thing that separates you from the naked edge of eternity is this knowledge and a few basic tools.

FIRST-AID KITS

The only tool you will carry specifically for emergencies is a first-aid kit. The kit you take along on your shakedown hike can be pretty basic: items taken from your medicine cabinet and folded into a waterproofed bag. The possibilities of a serious injury on a mild, four- to six-mile hike are fairly remote. However, as the length and difficulties of your backpacking trips expand, so must your kit. You might almost say that the conditions of your proposed hike should be directly proportionate to the size of your first-aid kit.

A basic trail overnight or weekend kit should contain at least the following items: gauze, adhesive tape, a couple of moderate pressure bandages, a few Band-aids, aspirin, elastic bandage, a bottle of water purification tablets (if necessary), snakebite kit (if necessary), and moleskins.

Longer trips, involving some off-trail hiking, should be reflected in the size and function of the kit. You will need more of everything in the trail kit plus a couple of four-by-five compresses, butterfly wound Band-aids, burn cream, antiseptic liquid or cream, and a good first-aid guide. Sierra West packages a trail kit for $6 and a Mountaineering kit for $11. There are several books available on wilderness and mountaineering medicine and there are any number of Red Cross publications on emergency care. Whichever book you buy, read it before you pack so you will at least know where to look in case of need.

Most of the equipment in your pack can also be brought to bear in an emergency. You can use your rope to construct a crude litter from pine saplings, covering it with a poncho or tent fly and wrapping the victim in sleeping bags. Before attempting to move any injured person, you ought to have some idea of the extent and nature of the injuries and what kind of movement is possible. Make sure your mountaineering medical guide book contains a good section on prognosis and care.

On your shakedown trip you can expect a number of minor "greenhorn" disasters, but nothing more. There may be scalded or burned fingers from the fire and cookware; a scraped shin or a minor cut on the arm from brush and rocks; perhaps a twisting of the old tennis knee or ankle (thus the pressure bandage). Other likely possibilities might be blistered or otherwise sore feet (remember the moleskins in time); sunburn (you forgot the cream); and maybe a touch of poison ivy (you know, the lovely three-leafed plant Junior picked at the start of the hike).

Those minor miseries you can expect and deal with in stride, but there are a host of other disasters waiting for you up there which you are going to have to recognize and learn to avoid. In the first place, make sure everybody is healthy at the start. Are there any aches or pains which could be the first signs of something really serious? Do you have any chronic conditions such as heart trouble or bronchitis that could flare up under stress? If you feel you are at the height of fitness, then the hike should be a pleasurable success.

While flying up the trail, watch out for rough landings. Hiking with a load on your back is not flying at all, it is the deliberate movement of one leg past the other. You should be conscious of every step you take and what the probable consequences are going to be. Walking down a paved sidewalk you can gaze at one another and look at the scenery, but on the trail, walking is your business and you had better keep your mind on it. When admiring the view, stop.

WATER

When you pitch camp, if not earlier along the trail, you are going to want a drink of water. Is it safe or are you going to have to boil it or purify it? This is one of the things you are going to have to know before setting out. Check with either the state conservation department, forester, or park ranger. If it is questionable, you had better play it safe. Follow the directions on your purification tablet container or boil it with a full minute's perk before drinking.

HAZARDS
Bugs

Bugs are a source of constant irritation in many areas but not a serious threat to health unless you are hiking in the Rocky Mountains during spotted-fever tick season or in arid environs of black widow spiders and scorpions.

Poisonous Vegetation

There are three species of plants in North America that can cause serious skin rashes with only minimal contact. They are the ubiquitous poison ivy, poison oak, and poison sumac. Poison ivy is found just about everywhere, although in some areas even abundant stands do not seem to be as potent as elsewhere. Poison oak and sumac are found generally in wet, lowland climates. Check ahead of time which of these you might find, and know how to identify them.

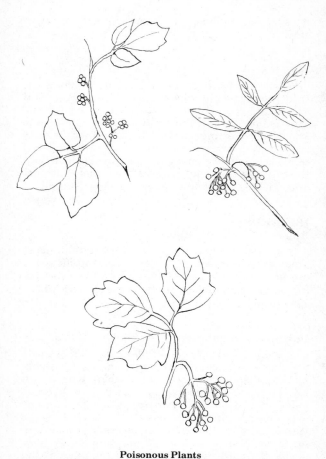

Poisonous Plants

Top left: Poison ivy. *Top right:* Poison sumac. *Bottom:* Poison
oak.

Animals

Wilderness contact with wild animals ranges from pure delight to absolute tragedy. The height of these experiences range generally in degree by the knowledge of animals and the species. The more you know about the animals you are likely to encounter, the higher your appreciation of them will be and the lower the risk.

It would be a dull hike indeed if your party didn't encounter at least a few four-legged furries. A deer bounding off through the forest waving its white tail goodby (or maybe beckoning you on); a pine squirrel chewing you out for disturbing him in his work; a marmot listlessly watching you from a boulder; or a beaver clapping the surface of its reservoir as you circumvent the flooded trail. These are some of the experiences that make all the work and sweat of backpacking a bargain. You aren't exactly seeing naked nature—all of those creatures have taken some kind of defensive or protective reaction because they know you don't really belong—but most wild animals will tolerate you at a distance.

Bears

There are some animals—bears—that occasionally will not tolerate human intrusions. Nearly all of the northern belt of states have bears. Over much of this range they are moderately large, black bears but in the Northern Rockies, between Glacier and Yellowstone National Parks, there still live the last of the great grizzly bears. Scientists call them *Ursus horribilis,* and you might take the cue. They are large, up to seven feet tall, and weigh as much as half a ton. They are solitary animals most of the year and move about as kings of their territory.

Bears

Top: Grizzly bear. *Bottom:* Black bear. Black bears are often colored light to dark brown, as is the grizzly. The latter can be distinguished, however, by its muscular hump and distinctive dished face.

In recent years there have been several sensational attacks in both national parks. Although the exact cause of the attacks seems to vary and is hard to pin down, park naturalists feel that these grizzlies have become contemptuous of human beings and regard us only as easy sources of food. Many attacks are caused by the victim attempting to stop a bear from stealing food. That's right—a 150-pound camper from Newark is mauled trying to defend the family crackers; it happens just about every year.

In 1967 two young women were killed in Glacier National Park by two separate sow grizzlies. The women were camped miles apart in highlands. Both women were in their menstrual cycles at the time and subsequent attacks under the same conditions have caused many naturalists to believe that menstrual discharge somehow sets off a territorial rage in sow grizzlies. Although there are no signs cautioning women about this possible danger in either park, rangers will discourage hiking in bear country during a period. There does not seem to be any evidence that this reaction exists with black bear sows.

Of course, the universal law of getting along with all animals, from ground squirrel to grizzly, is not to startle, tease, or corner them and not to get between a mother and her young. Nearly any animal will get its dander up under these conditions, but if you excite a bear, you have big problems.

To prevent problems with bears, make sure they know you are coming. Make a constant, human sounding noise such as singing or, better yet, have every member of the family wear bells. Bells and people sounds will, or course, reduce the possibility of other contact with wildlife, but in bear country the trade-off is probably worth it.

The aroma of either fresh or canned meats will attract bears—another good reason for not carrying these meats into the wilderness, and ample justification for catching only enough fish to eat immediately. The bears also provide a good excuse to keep your campsite clean, washing dishes, and burying dishwater right after dinner. If you have a campfire, burn all the leftover foods and use some of the dishwater to douse the fire. Your food bag should be kept high off the ground suspended between trees and all foods opened but not used should be tightly wrapped before storage. The bears will know you are there, even without food odors, but will probably not bother you unless they sense there is something in it for them.

Bears don't eat people. Virtually all attacks can be reduced to two motives: reaction to a threat or seeking an easy meal of people-food. In either case, the worst thing you can do is attempt to defend yourself or your property. Leading with your left or wielding a big stick will only make matters worse. If you see what appears to be an aggressive bear, freeze stock-still, wait for it to make the first move. If the standoff lasts very long, have everybody in your party gently remove their packs and lay them on the ground. Then start slowly backing away. If the bear does decide to attack, it may find what it wants before actually getting to soft flesh. If the bear attacks suddenly or during the staredown, try to get out of your packs and play dead. Ball up to protect your stomach and face and don't move. This may sound silly but it has saved many lives. The bear may take a swipe at you but will usually be quickly attracted to your pack.

Running is probably unwise but if you are going to break, go downhill where the bear is at least as

clumsy as you. You will never win an uphill race
with a bear.

Grizzlies can't climb trees, it is true, but remember they can reach up to ten feet so if you are
going to take to the branches, make sure you can get
higher than their reach by the time they get to the
tree. Black bears can shinny up any tree a lot faster
than you can and you will be much better off on the
ground.

Most of the time, encounters with bears end with
blacks high-tailing it in the opposite direction and
grizzlies making a dignified, slow retreat. In either
case don't push your luck; give them enough time to
swallow their humiliation or find someplace else to
go, or modify your plans by giving them a wide
berth. The best policy if attacked, if it isn't clear
above, is to ditch your pack and play dead. It is
probably unwise to get them any hotter or madder
than they already are by chasing you.

During the past sixteen years I have hiked exten-
sively in grizzly country and for the past four years I
have covered almost every square mile of their
range in the Western Montana Mission Mountains. I
have seen only two grizzlies and in each case the
bears sullenly retreated, leaving me in a kind of
humble, thankful awe. My closest experience—in
terms of distance and probably trouble—was west of
Waterton Park in Alberta. I was walking a thirty-
mile trail between the park and the north fork of the
Flathead River, without a care in the world. It was a
bright, fine day and I was singing my praise at
practically the top of my lungs. As I came around a
turn in the trail, I noticed some willows moving,
about twenty-five feet away, near a small stream. I
pulled up just as a wee brown ball of fur shot across
the creek and into dense cover on the other side. An

instant later a huge female grizzly reared up out of the bushes and gave me a quick side-long glance. She could have reached me in a matter of seconds but evidently decided that junior was safe and I probably wasn't worth the trouble, and stalked off behind her baby. When she had vanished into the brush, I backed off slowly around the corner, removed my pack, and sat down for a fairly long session about my place and hers in the universe.

As the amount of critical grizzly habitat is further shrunk by civilized progress, the handwriting on the wall for this magnificent creature becomes more apparent. Already, the once abundant creature is hemmed into a narrow 200-mile-long strip of high mountains and exists only by virtue of the inaccessibility of their territory. The territorial demand of each adult grizzly is so great that only a handful remain in this range. Recently, the grizzly has been declared "threatened" by the U.S. Fish and Wildlife Service and has been placed under federal protective management.

The two national parks that have grizzlies have been placed in a seemingly paradoxical situation of having to protect the dwindling population of bears while looking after the safety of the millions of human visitors every year. Current policy in both parks is to remove troublesome or "begging" bears to remote areas and condemn them to death if they return to their old habits. The problem with this management system is that no matter where a troublesome bear is taken, the territory is either going to be unsuitable or already occupied by another bear and one of them will be forced to return to begging and death.

Bears involved in attacks are relentlessly hounded down and killed, usually along with any innocent bear that happens to be in the neighborhood. And all this slaughter just to make this thin little wedge safe for that animal which dominates virtually every other square mile in the continental United States: us.

Americans have the blood of too many noble creatures on their conscience already. We have always gone into nature as conquerers and regarded her animals and resources on strictly human economic values. We have destroyed many of the former, exploited the latter, and left the land naked and defenseless. We now know that we can't go on doing this forever; we know that the world is not our plum, but a complicated system of ecological weights and balances which in the end involves our own well-being. We now have enough maturity that we know we can't continue to poison our own air, use the great lakes and oceans as cesspools, or flagrantly rip the guts out of the earth. Maybe it is time we also learn that we don't necessarily have to be the dominant species wherever we go—that there is room for other animals such as the grizzly to live in the way their habits dictate. In these places we should regard ourselves as visitors who have to obey the laws of the natives.

Grizzlies are one of the few things left to remind us that, stripped of our organization and material, we are after all, just animals, subject to the same laws of power and survival as other animals.

In the realm of the grizzly, black bears are meek and timid (which, of course, does not mean you can push them around). Here they are second-fiddle and are accustomed to giving ground. But outside the grizzly's range, black bears are lords of the wilderness and are not inclined to stepping aside for anything. Here they are more aggressive and self-

confident and should be given a wide sway when
encountered. If you are attacked, the same rules apply here as with the grizzly, although a lot of people
feel that bellicose blacks can be bluffed. Blacks can
weigh in at up to 500 pounds, so it would not ordinarily be an even contest toe-to-toe. A compromise
way to deal with a black might be to drop your pack,
back off a few steps and bluff quietly. He will
probably go away but even if he does pursue the
point, your pack may be of more interest than your
body.

Moose

The only other woodland wild animal that
can generally be considered potentially dangerous
within its range is the moose, especially a cow with
calves. Some oldtimers say they would rather run
into a bear with a cub than a mother moose. For my
own part, I have never seen a moose while I was
afoot and am looking forward to the first occasion.
Moose are fast but extremely dumb. Woodsmen say
that keeping a tree between you and their sharp
hooves is the best way of dealing with an attack.

Elk and possibly deer can be considered as
possibly dangerous, provided you go out of your way
to push them into action. If you see young of any
animal in the woods, leave it alone. Mother is
probably not far away and even if she is, young animals are not going to appreciate your attention.

Carrying a gun while backpacking is not only
illegal in many areas, but so utterly preposterous
that I am embarrassed to mention it. Nonetheless,
there is an occasional pistol-packing idiot in the
wilderness who should be regarded with more suspicion and caution than a PTA meeting of mother griz-

zlies and moose. The only damage a sidearm can possibly do to a large animal is to wound it and drive it mad with pain. Enraged, the animal will go like a hay mower through the imbecile that shot it and the other members in his party, as well as anybody else who might be in the neighborhood. A wounded bear is a danger to everybody and everything within his range and will remain so until someone puts it out of its misery. Gun-packers also tend to take great pleasure in shooting everything else that moves, which can easily include any slow-moving easy targets on two legs. The only thing you can do to protect yourself from these animals is let them know you are around and out of season and report them to authorities if they are in restricted areas.

Porcupines

There are other mammals which can create minor to major problems in hiking country but are not dangerous in a real sense. The most obvious of these is the porcupine.

The porkie is a slow, rather silly animal which has survived all this time chiefly by virtue of the sharp, painful quills it packs around its hips. If bothered, the porkie bristles its skirt of quills and leaves a few in anything or anybody foolish enough to be within range.

The porkie has another annoying trait which undoubtedly has contributed to its survival as a species: it will eat just about anything. As far as backpackers are concerned, its diet can and often does include boots, jackets, woolen clothing, fishing rod handles, cotton duck backpacks and even the door out of your tent.

The only way of protecting yourself from the

nocturnal porkie is to beware of his hind end and keep the more desirable cuisine out of reach or inside the tent. Also, a clean camp that doesn't smell of food won't be of much interest to him.

Skunks

Skunks, another nuisance beast, will probably also leave a clean camp alone. Skunks are justly famous for their unsavory emission and they will bite if pushed hard enough. And a skunk bite is not as funny as a skunk bath. Skunks carry any number of exotic diseases including rabies.

Small Mammals

Another potential animal problem that hiking parties with children ought to keep in mind is small mammals (such as rabbits) which are dead or dying or behaving in a peculiar manner. These animals could be infected with tularemia or other dangerous diseases which can be transmitted through skin contact. Make sure the children know that an apparently "tame" rabbit may be more dangerous than a lion.

Snakes

Snakes can also be a problem in most areas of the United States. There are poisonous snakes found in most areas but they are usually restricted to arid foothills or low-lying areas. In general, if you intend to hike in the deep South, you are going to have to watch out for cottonmouths, pigmy rattlers and coral snakes. Copperheads are found in the southeastern belt from Texas to Connecticut.

Timber rattlers are found throughout the South as far as upstate New York. From Texas to Michigan is the range of the tiny massasauga rattler. The prairie rattlesnake is found from Texas to Montana and the western diamondback rattler ranges from Texas into California.

Find out ahead of time which species you might encounter and try to get some idea of how common they are. You should be prepared with at least a snakebite kit and, if the distance and possible exposure to snakes is great enough, consider taking a syringe and anti-venom.

Exposure

Hypothermia, sometimes known as exposure, is a recently identified condition in which wet or overly-tired hikers lose the ability to generate heat as fast as they use it to moderate chills. If left untreated, a hiker can die quickly from the loss of essential body heat.

The usual conditions leading to hypothermia are sweaty or wet clothes from a hard hike losing their insulation value when cooler weather conditions set in. The victim usually does not recognize his plight because of a psychological inability to make judgment decisions. The lower the body temperature becomes, the less able the victim is to detect the problem, and it is more likely the condition will become fatal.

If you notice someone in your party begin to shiver uncontrollably, act in an irrational manner, or talk incoherently, take immediate measures. The hike should stop at once, even if a shelter or objective is very close. Set up a tent and wrap the victim in clothing and sleeping bags. If he doesn't show improvement immediately, he should be warmed by somebody else's body.

The only way to positively avoid hypothermia is to stay dry and as warm as is necessary to remain comfortable under current weather conditions. This means changing sweaty or rain-wetted clothing immediately and keeping your head warm by wearing a wool cap or other appropriate headgear.

Getting along in the wilderness is primarily a matter of developing faith in your own knowledge and resources rather than relying on the network of social technology. This means you are going to have to learn to recognize problems, know how to avoid them, and have the skill and confidence to deal with them if they become serious.

Remember to watch where you are walking—what or whom you might be walking into, and strictly obey the laws of the management and creatures in the land you are visiting. Above all, use your head first, and if things go wrong, remember to keep it.

CHAPTER SEVEN

Directions

If you plan to hike and camp on a well-established trail during your shakedown outing—and you probably should—why bring along a map and compass? After all, it is probably as hard to get lost on a worn footpath as on an interstate highway, right?

Right and wrong. When you are driving along a highway you don't really know exactly where you are most of the time, all you know is that you are on a lateral line between wherever you started and wherever it is you want to go. You orient yourself along the way with landmarks, usually towns. The last town you passed was forty miles from the next town and when you get to it, you will have an exact idea of your location. But when you leave you will be traveling down that geometric nether-zone of a line between two points.

In trail hiking, you are going to want to know
more than where to start and where to end. You are
going to require some notion of location and progress
along the way and accurately identify your camping
objective at the end of the day. You are also going to
want to assure yourself that you are on the right
trail. It is easier to get sidetracked on a game path
than to make a wrong turnoff on a highway, and
how many times have you taken exit fifty-six when
you wanted exit sixty-five?

MAPS

A map is unquestionably one of your most essential pieces of equipment. The maps available
from the U.S. Geological Survey are either fifteen-
minute, large area maps, or 7.5–minute detailed
scale. Elevation lines—those wiggly ripples all over
the map—are probably set in either forty-foot intervals or 100-foot intervals. To find out how much
vertical climb these contour intervals represent,
look at the bottom of the map where you will also
find the scale and the date the map was checked for
accuracy.

The symbols you will need to know for orientation
are trails, which are dashed black lines; lakes,
which are solid blue; and streams, which are represented by blue lines.

The squiggly ripple elevation marks are red except where they pass through marshes or glaciers.
On most 7.5-minute maps fine red lines represent
forty-foot intervals separated every 200 feet by
heavier red lines which every now and then have
elevation marks written into the line. To under-
stand these lines, think of them as layers. You will

notice, if you look near a high point on the map, that these lines are actually bent-out-of-shape circles which come together at some point. Each of the distorted circular layers rests upon the lower circle, usually with distinct margins between the two. This distance is the lip of the higher layer over the preceding one.

Obviously, the lay of the land does not conform to the forty-foot-high steps inferred in the map. This would mean that mountains were shaped exactly like stacks of coins with 50¢ pieces on the bottom and dimes on the top. Instead, these steps represent forty-foot ripple marks on a sloping hill with the distance between the lines on the map showing the pitch or grade of the hill at that point. If the lines on the map are very close together, it means the pitch is very steep. If they are fairly far apart on the map, it indicates a more gradual slope. If you find the lines on your map bunched together near your route, you know that at that point along your hike, you will see a very steep cliff. You can measure the height of the cliff by counting the contour lines that bunch together and multiplying by forty.

Large mountains are usually identified on the summit in black printing with the elevation inscribed in red. Lakes also often have the elevation inscribed in dark blue. These are handy landmarks which can give you an idea of where you are and, sometimes, where you ought not to be.

Now, lay the map out on a table; it measures slightly more than two feet high by slightly less than two feet wide. In a standard 7½-minute quadrangle you will find an area about ten miles by six miles represented in the map. Sometimes you will have to order and carry two adjoining maps to cover the extent of your hike.

MAP PLANNING

Find your trail and follow it through from trail-head, where you will begin and probably end the hike, to your farthest destination. You have already estimated the distance (and a rough estimate is all you are going to get because even highly accurate topos usually cut off small switchbacks or bends in the trail), and you also know the vertical climb (the elevation from the trailhead to your ultimate destination). You have also calculated approximately how long a leisurely pace will get you from trailhead to camp (by allowing an hour for every mile and an additional hour for every 1,000 feet vertical climb), so that your route is planned and your destination is located within the amount of time you have available for the hike.

Now, while you are finger-walking the map, locate some landmarks along the route that you will be able to identify when on the trail. These can be waterfalls, stream crossings, lakes, steep cliffs near the trail, long switchbacks, marshes, prominent ridges or high peaks. If you are going to use peaks for orientation, make sure they aren't going to be obscured by closer ridges and hills. Also look for branches in the trail (they won't all show up on a topo map), and make sure that you know which way you are supposed to be going.

Now you have a series of landmarks to act as road signs for you on the trail. If you have a road sign every quarter- to half a mile, that will probably be sufficient to keep you reasonably secure about your direction. But this is usually not the case. Trails have a way of changing yearly while maps change only every decade or so. Any of the thousands of morphological systems that are common in nature—landslides, avalanches, beaver ponds, streams taking on new channels, trees falling, and animals walking—are constantly working on the direction of trails, while it often takes a basic land-use modification to alter a map. When you are out in the wilderness you should have another more reliable and accurate method of orienting yourself and your map to the terrain.

COMPASS

Compasses have been used for centuries to indicate direction, and if you know how to use one and have a map, it is almost impossible to lose your way. The problem is to get the map and the compass working together for you.

Compasses come in two basic styles: There is the older military and surveyor's quadrant compass and the new azimuth type. The quadrant compass was designed for mapmakers who were trained in a lot of complicated math to measure distances accurately within an inch. The azimuth compass was designed to do the same thing, with tolerances broadened to a few feet, for anybody who can add and subtract. There are two modestly priced and excellently designed azimuth compasses available almost anywhere today. The Silva compass system is basically a revolving compass housing on a transparent base. The base has an etched line-of-direction arrow and a ruled straight edge along both sides. Silva compasses start under $5 for a non-liquid filled housing model. Another several dollars will buy a liquid-filled model which adds not only quick reading but also a certain amount of shock insulation to the housing. Other models run up to about $25.

Finnish made Suunto compasses are similar in

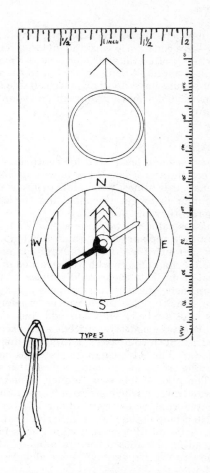

Basic Azimuth Compass with Clear Base and Straight Edge

design to Silvas but have a wider range of prices. The basic, liquid-filled, rotating-head model costs about the same, but other models with elaborate sighting devices and housings range up to $45.

If you have an old compass surviving your Boy Scout days or grandpa's stint in the cavalry, it will probably do, but it will be harder to use with a map than the transparent-based compasses.

The basic function of any compass is to find north. The magnetic needle will do this, without any urging from you, provided there is no metallic or magnetic interference nearby. Once north is known, the other directions or degrees can be easily determined on any compass.

THE MAP, THE COMPASS, AND THE LANDSCAPE

Although a compass is a handy tool by itself, when combined with an accurate topo map it is better than a filling station for finding directions. To get the two working together, you must first orient your map so that its indicated north corresponds to actual north from where you are standing. Line the map to magnetic north by holding the compass against a meridian line of the map and adjust them until everything is pointed north. Now compensate the map and compass for the magnetic declination (the difference between magnetic north and true north), which you will find at the bottom of your topo map. If your map says the declination is twenty degrees east, turn the map twenty degrees in the opposite direction.

Now to figure out where you are—besides sitting out in the middle of nowhere with a tired, hungry family wanting to know what declination and bear-

ings have to do with dinner. There is a peak visible
on your right. You know by looking at your map that
it is Warden Mountain. Sight along the true-north-
oriented compass until you can fairly accurately determine the degree of direction Warden is from you
at this point. Let's say it is ninety degrees. Now, look
off to your left—there in the distance is McDonald
Peak. Sight along your compass until you are confident you know the bearing (degree of direction), of
McDonald. Hypothetically we call McDonald 270
degrees.

Now, without moving the map from its oriented
position, remove the compass, and line the straight
edge so that it touches Warden Peak and draw a line
from the peak of Warden ninety degrees to a point
which should intersect with your location. Turn the
straight edge around so that it touches McDonald
Peak and draw a line 270 degrees until it crosses
your Warden azimuth. The intersection of the two
lines is your present position. Wow, less than a mile
to go!

This method of navigation is called triangulation,
and it works fine as long as you have two known im-
movable points to draw bearings from. What do you
do, however, if the landscape does not provide any
prominent points (in flat, featureless country, in a
dense wood, or in a thick overcast)? Knowing exactly
where you are may be nice to reduce anxieties but if
you are on or near a trail, being able to pinpoint
your precise location on the map is not a matter of
survival. If you can find the trail, you can find your
way out.

If you do leave the trail, you are probably doing so
for some good reason—a hidden lake over a ridge
perhaps. Examine your map to determine the easiest route to the lake. When you come to your demar-

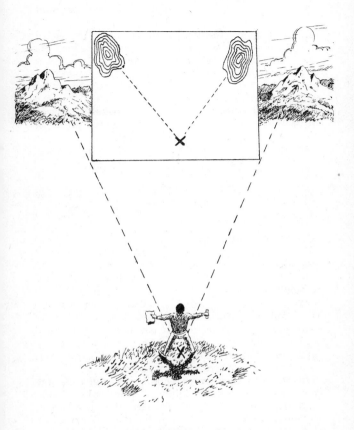

Triangulating Location

Take bearings on two known points, such as mountain peaks, lakes or other landmarks. Transpose the bearings onto your map by drawing a line from each point to your approximate location. Where the two lines meet is your precise location.

kation point on the trail—which you will have to
recognize either by a prominent feature along the
trail or triangulation—take a bearing on your route
to the lake. If, at any time along the way, you have
to deviate from the bearing, make a note of the
degree of deviation.

With your overland line to the lake recorded, you
can easily find your way back to the trail even in the
gloomiest of fogs by merely taking a back-bearing.
This means that if you left the trail taking a course
of forty-five degrees north by northeast, you would
return by a course of 225 degrees south by south-
west. And don't forget to back-line around any deviation you took going to the lake.

Overland Route

Another sound idea and a practice which is almost
second nature to any seasoned woodsman or mountaineer, is to determine the fastest overland course
to safety before you actually start the trip. Where,
for instance, is the nearest heavily traveled road and
what general direction will this be from the route of
your hike? In deciding on an overland general
course, make sure there are no obstacles such as
large lakes, high mountain ridges, or cliffs that
would prevent you from getting through.

In the unlikely event that you should become
inexorably lost, merely follow the general direction
of your preplanned overland route. If you continue,
say, on a north bearing, you will eventually run into
the east-west highway skirting the wilderness area
in which you are hiking. Using your compass when
lost will at least force you to hold a steady course
and overcome the natural tendency of most people to
run around in circles.

Compasses are critical enough to the emergency welfare of the party that every member should have one. Each member, even children who will presumably be with adults during the entire hike, should also have a rudimentary notion of what compasses are all about. This means knowing the overland route formula and how to take bearings and return on them. Having an abundance of compasses will also prevent the possibility of being stuck someplace in the wilds without the compass that slipped off your neck two miles back, or a broken one.

A good compass is impervious to rain or dunkings, but a map is not. Package your map in a plastic bag and store it under easily accessible cover in your pack. Most packs have special map pockets in the flap. Fold it in the same direction after every use or soon you will have eight small maps instead of the one you started with. Some people regard the integrity of the map as being important enough to warrant backing it with a lightweight nylon fabric.

CHAPTER EIGHT

Last-minute Preliminaries

INFORMATION

Before setting out, make sure you have all the basic information you are going to need to organize your nomadic lives for the next day or two. You already know the general regulations and rules in the area from talking with conservation department biologists or game wardens or forest and park service rangers. You should also ask them about the condition of the trail—whether or not you can expect some hard spots; animals you might watch for; insects; and the odds on rain or snow. On your way to the trailhead, you might stop at a sporting goods store or service station and find out what tidbits of local lore they will impart. When you are starting or on the trail, exchange greetings and swap scuttlebutt with any hikers you may pass. Don't be afraid to ask questions.

Weather

The whims of the weather always affect the welfare of a hiking party. Foul, cold, wet weather can affect your well-being and will most certainly leave a lasting impression—or depression—on novice parties. Weather in the mountains is famous for its caprice. A fine sunshine can turn into a dour rain with incredible alacrity and timing. And when mountains get socked in, they normally stay that way longer than the lowlands.

A lofty mountain range presents a geological barrier known as a rain shelter to incoming storms. Low pressure areas that move quickly across flatter areas literally get stuck on the mountains.

Steep river valleys, such as the Grand Canyon and the Colorado River gorge, can become a nightmare of savage elements in a flash storm. A gentle flow can rise to a torrent in a matter of minutes, taking everything in its way. Marshy areas, such as much of Michigan's Upper Peninsula and the northern Midwest, can become quagmires overnight in a heavy rain. Hilly, low, mountain terrain such as the Adirondacks and the New England belts have enormous rainfalls which tend to sneak in after you have put a lot of trail behind you.

Each meteorological zone in the U.S. has its own equally unreliable system of seat-of-the-pants weather forecasting. In the West, for instance, it is never supposed to rain until the barometer has hit bottom and has started up. Conversely, in the East rain is normally expected on lowering barometric pressure.

Reading Cloud Makeup

Characteristics of clouds and the sky are often regarded as ways of predicting changes in the weather. Obviously a thick slate-gray sky portends showers but you can also get some idea of a change for the worse from high nimbus clouds with a lower tier of strata clouds moving beneath. Many woodsmen look for variations in the shades of clouds and will take cover when different levels of clouds are moving in opposite directions.

Mountaineers apply the atmospheric moisture rule to a view of their favorite places, the mountains. They say that if you can stand back ten miles from the mountains and distinguish minute detail and color, there is no haze and therefore little likelihood of rain.

The direction and form of campfire smoke is another way of predicting the shape of things to come. An easterly wind, for instance, often means wet or even foul weather. If the smoke rises thinly straight up, you can leave the flap of your tent open because you are in a high-pressure zone. However, if the smoke trickles along the ground in one direction or another or just hangs over the fire in a low mist, batten up because the pressure is low and something is moving in.

Many people are blessed (they may say "cursed"), with weather-sensitive joints, nerves, or muscles. A woman I know gets aching shoulders and neck when the weather stabilizes, and one of my best hiking companions can foretell rain with remarkable accuracy from a pain in his knee. Another friend had a nerve in his jaw severed during the war and predicts storms by a tingling in his teeth. He is almost always right.

Perhaps the most reliable way that experienced

devotees of the wilds divine the weather is by turning on the radio the evening before an excursion,
and double-checking the forecast again as they are
packing in the morning. If you have a hard time
tuning in the radio through the crackle and pop
of static, it means there is atmospheric distur-
bance or lightning and possibly foul weather ahead.
Whether or not gloomy forebodings will delay the
trip depends on the individuals and the amount of
time available.

SEARCH AND RESCUE

Most communities around wilderness areas have
search and rescue squads or volunteer deputy pa-
trols organized to clean up lost hikers in the bush.
Find out whom to contact and a number where he or
they can be reached. Write the number down on a
piece of paper, fold it around a coin for a pay
telephone, and give an additional copy to everybody
in the party. You have already established a cross-
country escape route. Now note the closest telephone
to the trailhead and make sure everybody knows
where it is.

It is wise to check in with the search-and-rescue
squad, sheriff's department, or ranger headquarters
and give them your complete backpacking itinerary.
Tell them where you expect to go, how you expect to
get there and when you will be returning. You
might even leave them a dated map with your route
penned in. And don't forget to check back when you
return.

LEAVING WORD

You might also want to leave a map and schedule
with neighbors or friends at home.

If you do run into a problem in the hills, knowing that somebody will soon be looking for you can be quite reassuring. Help is not around the corner, as it would be back in the cradle of civilization, but it is only a day or so away. If you can't hike out, but manage to keep warm, dry, and in control of yourself and your party, you won't have any trouble getting through a couple of nights.

CARS

The last lap, getting from the outskirts of civilization to the trailhead, has become a real problem in recent years. You can drive up and leave your car at whatever parking space is available but this is increasingly risky. Nearly every community has its local cadre of fun-lovers or rip-off artists who know that hikers have to leave their vehicles abandoned in remote, isolated parking lots. With all the time in the world and a few simple tools, they can either trash your car beyond recognition or strip it of all marketable parts. Many of those shiny hubcaps that studded the walls of the secondhand store back in town may have come from parked cars like yours.

A friend of mine left Missoula a while back for a week-long trek through Western Montana's majestic Bitterroot Mountains. He left his car in a campground above a small, decent, conservative rural community and set off on a long loop which would take him into some of the Idaho Selway's best and back again. Forty miles, ten pounds, and seven days later he wobbled the last mile to his trusty station wagon. Most of the wagon was still there. About all he could find missing were the tires, battery, electrical parts, and gas (which he really didn't need by that point anyway). Whoever got to it did a fairly neat, professional job except they broke both side windows and slit the upholstery in the process. My friend Ken took his last swallow of water and wrath and stumbled two more miles to the nearest farmhouse.

He was probably lucky. It seems that backpacking is tougher on stationary cars than on wandering hikers. I know of others who have had the family chariot stolen, rolled into lakes, used as a target or wantonly smashed while waiting for its owners.

There are several things you can do to avoid risking your car during your hike, and locking it is not one of them. Sometimes there are buses from the nearest community which travel by the trailhead. It is unlikely that you will get as close as you would with the car but a short extra hike may be worthwhile. Bus stations often have fairly secure parking facilities. If not, try a service station or ask the police if you can leave it near headquarters. If you are going to take a bus be sure you know what the return schedule is. You could find yourself bag and baggage on the roadside until two a.m.

Another possibility is to either have a friend or gas station attendant drive you up and return on schedule to retrieve you. Going a long way out of the way is a pretty large favor to ask of a stranger and it will probably cost you, but you can think of it as damage insurance on your car.

For people who hike a lot and live fairly close to the wilderness, there is a third alternative: Leave a far-from-virgin sacrifice to the clods.

I live five road-miles from my favorite stamping grounds and have a total radius of operations of about fifty miles, or twenty-five miles to my farthest trailhead. Every year or two, depending on how lucky I am, I spend $50 to $75 on a still-running junker. Appearances are really important in a "sacrifice car" so I look around carefully for a heap that appears not to have more than five downhill miles left in it and offer nothing more to the discriminating thief than the possibility of a few good cigarette butts in the ashtray. I have lost a little gas but have found that there are levels below which even the meanest of creatures will not crawl.

If the sacrifice-car route appeals to you, there are a couple of considerations you should take into account. Be sure that time and miles in the old goat are not going to accomplish what has been denied to the thieves. A flat tire or two or a dead battery can extend your hike beyond the point of healthful weariness as surely as a stolen car. I resolve the former ticket to sore feet by carrying a good spare and making sure the four on the road are at least moderately worthy. Batteries are awfully expensive and easier to pick from a car than tires so I resolve this potential problem by always parking on enough of an incline to "run-start."

And the old clunker is your responsibility until it earns its final rest as a rectangle of compressed metal. If it dies with your boots on, you are legally and morally responsible for seeing to it that it is hauled out of the woods and to the dump. Remember the tin-can principle.

You now know everything you can know ahead of time to assure the safety and comfort of the party; your gear is assembled and ready, and you are on the way to the trailhead. Now come the first steps in earnest.

CHAPTER NINE

Starting Out

ON THE TRAIL

Fitting, adjusting, balancing, and distributing packs and loads for the party should be the last act before finally setting off on the trail.

This could be done at home, and in fact some of it should·be, but it is best to field-fit and test your equipment after you are dressed and in the mood, right at the trailhead. You are not only able to adjust for the exact conditions, but you also cut down on the amount of stuffed time for your down bag and jacket and get more equitable and comfortable distribution of loads.

Adjusting and Distributing Loads

Obviously, loads should be divided on a diminishing scale of largest to smallest hiker, but nobody should be overburdened.

When adjusting a load within a pack, it is generally best to concentrate most of the heavy objects in the lower back. Any room in your pack below is usually reserved for the sleeping bag, and the upper portions of the pack can be stuffed with light, soft things such as clothing or jackets. The very top of everybody's pack should be set aside for trail-handy items you are not going to want to dig out while on the hike. These include GORP, canteens, usable hiking clothing such as shorts and waterproofs. The map should be kept handy in the lid of somebody's pack along with binoculars or camera. Compasses should be carried in pockets along with knives.

Some packs, especially soft and integral frames, are awkward under poorly balanced loads, and it doesn't take any princess to feel a pea in these. Make sure the area of the pack which will come in direct contact with hips, back, and shoulders is free from hard objects. Lay a pair of pants or a jacket vertically up the back of the pack before stuffing in hard goods.

A sleeping bag, extra clothing, and a few this-and-thats will fit nicely into a child's daypack, but be sure that spoons and cups are not against the back, and that one side of the pack is as heavy as the other.

External framepacks are a little easier to arrange because the pack is set away from your back. But again, carrying is easier if you stash the heavy things in the bottom of the bag close to the back, with the bagged sleeping bag tied on below, and lighter things stuffed in the sack above.

Balancing the load in one of the new columned softpacks is really critical. Well packed, they are little more bother than the shirt on your back but a listing load completely destroys their advantages.

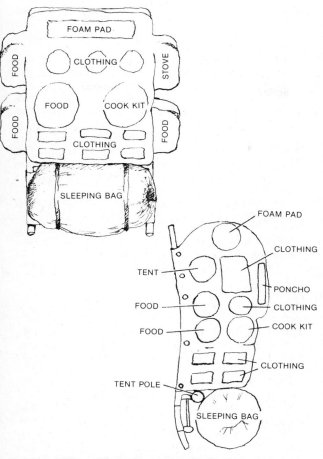

Well-adjusted Load on External Frame Pack
The weight is even from side to side and concentrated against the back.

Size everything up carefully before stuffing it down one of the vertical columns.

Now that everybody is loaded and at least stoically content with their respective loads, make sure the packs are fitting well. Shoulder straps should be snug enough to bring the top of the pack up over the shoulders but not so tight as to cut off circulation to the arms. Waist belts should ride along the tops of the hips. The shoulders should be hunched or the bottom of the pack lifted before the belt is tightened. Keep the belts snug—they are there to displace some of the weight that will be falling on your shoulders.

Most external frames and many soft and integral frame packs, have shoulder-to-belt length adjustments. If, when the pack is loaded and shoulder straps drawn, the belt rides too high or too low, make the appropriate adjustments.

Pace

Now you are going to have to develop a pace everyone can maintain on an uphill hike with loaded packs. You want to get to your overnight camping objective without wearing anyone out, which means a party gait comfortable to the slowest member.

Children have a tendency to start off extremely fast and end the day extremely slow. If you think Junior is pushing a little too hard at the outset, slow him down.

Pace is the sum of uphill and level ground stride times the frequency and length of stops. On your first hike you should plan on several short stops, say, one-minute breathers every fifteen minutes or so. You will also want a fifteen-minute lunch break and perhaps longer munching or drinking breathers every now and then. If, however, you find the party stopping too often and staying too long, there is something wrong with the stride. Slow it down until the party can continue merrily along its way with only scheduled stops. By scheduled stops, I don't mean every fifteen minutes the party drops where they are to stare at one another, but regular stops, say between ten and thirty minutes, when something worth looking at comes along. You are up there to tantalize your senses and a well-measured pace should allow plenty of leisure to drink up the sights.

Stride

Stride is like a normal walking step except it is more deliberate. Without a load, walking is second nature to most people. The speed of a walking pace is usually governed by the needs of the moment.

A stride, on the other hand, is a weight-adjusted step calculated to get you from point A to point B within the allotted amount of time. It is composed of the length and tempo of the step and should be balanced between the two. The step should be as long as possible without allowing the weight of the pack to throw you off balance at the top of the step with as quick a tempo as the traffic will bear.

Walking is actually deliberately throwing yourself off balance by leaning your center of gravity too far forward and regaining balance by bringing the swing foot forward under the off-balance lead. Human beings are actually the only animals that use the weight of their bodies to create a forward momentum that the legs have only to keep up with. Strange as it may sound, the weight of a pack actually increases the natural momentum of your body when you are walking on the level or downhill. There is a negative trade-off in this formula in the body energy required to balance and maintain the level of the pack, but there is no question that the pack generates an awful lot of forward momentum (as you will discover the first time you step on a wobbly rock while going downhill).

The point is to use your pack as much as possible in your stride. Don't bend way over into the trail because your back and shoulders are going to have to recover the weight of the pack after every step. Rather, keep your back straight with your head just slightly ahead of the foot that is carrying the weight. Be sure to know exactly where the swing foot is going to land and what kind of reception it can expect. Also, since you are building up momentum with every step, you might as well hold it as long as possible with a smooth, easy stride.

Uphills are another problem. Your legs are pushing your weighted foot forward and up with every step so don't give them more to do than is really necessary. The swing foot should just barely clear the ground after leaving the toe and the end of the stride should land as lightly as possible on your heel. If there is an obstacle in the path try to swing your foot or body around it. Don't climb anything, even a three-inch-high rock, if you don't have to.

When you come to an incline, slow down. Remeasure your pace to the pitch and difficulty of the trail. Don't try to iron everything to the same pace because you will end up depleted and decreased.

One way of structuring an easy pace for everybody in the party is to keep a moving conversation going. If somebody starts breaking sentences into three or four long pauses, you might slow things down a bit.

Breaks

Breathers should be just that: Brief stops to catch
your breath or let your breath be taken away by a
view. Removing and replacing packs requires a lot of
time and energy so you may as well leave them on
and just lean against a tree or sit on a log.

A water or snack stop can be a little more leisurely. If shoulders are getting tired, give them a
rest by taking off packs. Sit around, let your lungs
catch up with you, have a spot of water and splash in
the face (if there is ample water available). Don't sit
around too long, though, because after about ten
minutes muscles begin to stiffen, and getting started
again is tough.

Lunchbreak. As we said before, lunches on the
trail are a bit more casual than the organized affairs
down below. There is no whistle and no long wind-
down before you get back to the grind. Trail breaks
are just brief stops when everybody agrees that a little refreshment might be nice for the stomach. You
can haul out the GORP and powdered milk for a
cereal in your cup—or just GORP out of the bag—or,
if you please, a spot of hot bouillon heated over your
stove might go well.

Your party might be ready for such a stop every
couple of hours or you can break for just one meal on
the trail.

Everytime you take your pack off you might try a
map exercise. See if you can locate your stop on the
map by the view you are enjoying or trail features
you noticed a little way back. Think you are looking
out over Pat's Point, ah? Well, check your seat-of-
pants-navigation with a triangulation. Chances are
your original reckoning was right but you need the
practice anyway.

There is also an object lesson to be learned. You are going to notice something peculiar about this insignificant piece of cerebral exercise: you. Remembering how to go about it will be tougher than you expected and even recalling, from one moment to the next, the degrees of your bearings will be a strain. The fact is, you are literally dumber than you were when you left (which explains a lot about mountaineers). Oxygen and blood sugars that are fueling your brain during your normal sedentary life are now being used to fire your muscles and other organs. Don't worry, it isn't permanent. Your "smarts" will come trickling back in a few minutes but you should take note of the phenomena. When you try to think on your feet from the trail, you are likely to make mistakes. If you find yourself in a situation where some hard problem must be solved, sit down and digest it for a few minutes. Think it over once, then rest and think it over again. In order to keep your head on the trail you have to first recover it.

Stream Crossings

Most worthwhile trails are mixtures of interesting features. These trail features, while making the walking of them an exciting experience, can occasionally present problems. That babbling brook or spellbinding waterfall may sometime cross the trail and there isn't a bridge you are going to have to cross when you come to it.

Most trails lead over fords, or easy-to-cross areas of the streams. Few will take you through the stream above or below waterfalls or in the middle of a cascade or steep drop. If the current isn't too strong and the depth no higher than the knees of the shortest hiker, a refreshing wade will be a welcome change of pace.

Wet hiking boots may be worse than no boots at all for a backpacker. They are an open invitation to blisters and welcome all manner of fungi and other undesirables to attack your feet. Therefore, before fording the stream, take a break on the near shore. Have a drink of cool water (if you are sure it is safe), and change into tennis shoes and shorts. If somebody forgot the tennis shoes, cross over, then send a pair back across or have that person wade in socks (some people can actually wade gravel streams in bare feet but I don't know how). Remember while leading the party across that the only thing on earth more slippery than a wet, moss-covered rock is a wet, naked log. Smaller members may need a hand to cross, which will probably mean two trips for the adults—one for packs and one for children.

If the stream is too high or deep to wade safely, use your rope (that 100 feet of quarter-inch braided nylon coiled in the middle of the pack). Tie or have a couple of the party strongly belay (which is essentially the same thing as anchoring in a tug-of-war), and tie the other end around your waist. Move carefully across, angling with the current. If you should lose your balance, the rope will pull you back to the shore.

Once across, fasten or belay the rope so the others can start sending packs across ship-to-ship lifeline style. Then the other members can cross using the rope as a hand line. The last crosser, who should be the second strongest in the party, will have to angle across anchored to the far shore the same as the first member was anchored to the near shore. Change into dry clothes (or if conditions and the relationship of the party permit, don't bother wearing any on the crossing), and you are on your way again.

Rock

Some mountain trails have rock pitches or ledge trails which, although certainly not difficult, may make some members of a novice party feel better with a rope around their waists. Quarter-inch rope, which has a breaking strength of about 1,600 pounds, will not stop a dead fall of an adult. However, it will stop a sliding fall of anybody. If you want to rope in an entire party over a sliding slope you should have thirty feet of rope between each member which means one 100-foot rope will handle three people. An easy way to fit ropes on three persons is to double-knot three-foot-diameter loops at each end. The two largest people on the rope should tie the loop around their waists draped with a non-slipping knot such as a bowline knot. The person in the middle merely doubles the line around his waist and ties a nonslipping knot. Remember loose rock, and don't look down.

Walking up trails with steep pitches and some fall exposure should not really be walking at all; rather, each foot should be firmly placed and secure before the swing foot is moved. If the pitch is steep enough, you might have to use your hands as well, but remember that feet are much more reliable than hands. They can easily bear the weight of your entire body while handholds should be regarded only as a way of maintaining balance.

The tendency when walking on a thin trail looking straight down at the scenery is to lean into the pitch with your feet pushed away from your body. If

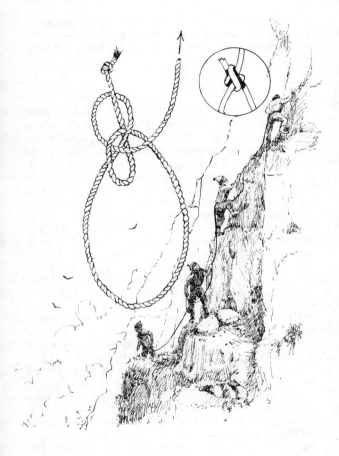

Bowline Knot
This knot is good for roping in on a steep trail.

you think about it, it is obvious that the center of
your weight should be placed directly over your feet.
Fight that inclination to list, and bring your body
directly over your feet.

Snow

The higher you go into mountains, even in mid-
summer, the greater the odds of running into a
snowfield or glacier. Most trails wisely avoid them
but if you find the trail disappearing into a late
patch of snow, you are going to have to deal with it.
If the snow is on a pitch, the best way to deal with it
is to go around. Hard, steep snow is one of the most
treacherous traveling conditions in the mountains.

If the patch is flat or has a soft but firm surface,
you can cross it but only with care. On a pitch, you
might want to rope up again and you will certainly
want to protect your boots from wet slush. This is
where the gaiters we talked about earlier will come
in handy. If your hike is going to take you into summer snow country, you will surely want a pair for
everybody.

Kick steps into the snow with the heel of your boot
before resting your foot. If the snow is too hard to
break the surface or too soft to hold a step, you would
be wise to get off the pitch and walk around.

The odds against running into an unavoidable
snowfield during the summer are so remote it is
hardly worth worrying about. However, if your map
is marked with glaciers near the trail or you discover ahead of time that icefields are still hanging
on the slopes along your intended route, you might
be wise to change your plans. Glaciers, icefields, and
sloping snow require special equipment (such as an
ice ax) and specialized knowledge.

Camp

Now the trail, with all its hidden charms and pit-falls, is behind you and the party has reached its overnight objective. Most trails are altogether too well provided with adequate camping sites so you will probably have no trouble locating a satisfactory spot. There are two ways of looking at site selection and both of them recognize fundamental requirements. Many of the new consciousness hikers feel that campsites that have apparently been used previously should be avoided. They argue that compacted earth, defoliation and charred firepits will not recover unless they are left fallow for a couple of seasons. They are right. Heavily used spots break up the harmony of the wilderness and require a lot of time to become restored.

The other group seeks out established sites. They maintain that a well-cared-for campsite every mile or so along a well-used trail does not materially add to the civilizing of the trail and point out that the use of virgin sites always causes some damage. They feel that a few good sites kept clean are preferable to a number of lightly used pioneer camping areas. They also point out that total recovery of a site with a heavily used firepit may take many years even though a cosmetic growth of plants may appear after a couple of seasons.

The choice is more or less academic, depending on whether a site is available where you decide to pull up for the night, and personal preference. However, if you intend to build a small cooking fire—large bonfires are now in total disrepute because of the damage they do to surrounding trees and the unconscionable waste of fire fuels—by all means seek out an existing pit.

Both sides of the campsite issue agree that living

things on the trail and around the camping place should be religiously respected and that nothing should be cut or trampled unless it is unavoidable. The days of greenwood fires, bough-covered-sapling lean-tos, reclining camp furniture, and uptown toilets are dead and should be put to rest. If you can't do without them, you might as well stay home. The trees and the undergrowth are all part of that priceless commodity we call wilderness which gives these lands an alternative value to economic exploitation. The loss of every tree or bush detracts from the ethereal value side of the ledger and makes it easier for those who manage the lands to emphasize the economic value of the resources.

These arguments notwithstanding, there are a number of objective criteria for a safe, cozy, and comfortable campsite. Obviously, your party is going to need enough relatively flat, smooth ground for pitching shelters or tents. The ground does not have to be perfectly level nor does it have to be contiguously large enough for all shelters to stand in a row. The army may insist on that kind of rank-and-file order in their bivouacs but hikers should seek to avoid it. Nature seldom follows straight lines and a row of neatly lined tents looks out of place in the wilderness.

You are also going to need water—which might be your first consideration—but there are different ways of looking at the convenience of leaning back from the fire and dipping it from a lake. Lakes and streams, because they are normally warmer than the ambient evening air, have a way of attracting the coldest air around. They also catch or generate winds and breezes.

There are two ways of looking at cold nights. They can stifle the late evening chatter around the campfire and make getting up early in the morning a heroic endeavor on the one hand. The other side of the coin presents a material reduction in nighttime and morning insect pests, as well as making cooler sleeping conditions.

Breezes do about the same thing: combined with a lakeside chill, they can reduce the insulating value of a sleeping bag by disturbing the dead air but they also help keep flying insects away.

Hillside pockets above the water are usually warmer and stiller, the conditions mosquitoes and some biting gnats seek.

I like a waterside camp. I prefer to sleep outside (but find swatting mosquitoes all night distinctly unrestful), and I seem to sleep better with a cool breeze on my face. I also find the celebrated somnolent attributes of running water a real asset to dropping off. I have also discovered that when cheery conversation drifts off into shivers, turning in for a good night's sleep is much easier.

You will also want some kind of shelter around the camp to break a strong evening wind. A rock ledge or a cove of small evergreens will do nicely, but be careful of large trees, which can attract lightning and drop branches on your camp; and don't pitch where rocks might tumble from a hill or ledge.

Pitching

If you arrive at your destination and locate a campsite early enough to go fishing or swimming, you might want to wait until you have established at least a minimal camp. No matter how inviting the water looks, you are probably going to be setting up some of your gear for the first time and it will go more quickly in the broad daylight.

Shelters should be first because they are normally
the most mechanically demanding and require the
greatest care in site selection. Locate smooth, rock-
and debris-free patches which will be at least hori-
zontally level (so tentmates aren't rolling into each
other all night). If there is a mild vertical pitch,
stake the front of the tent on the high side. If you
intend to make a fire, be sure the tents are located
well away from the pit to avoid damage from sparks
and cinders. Don't rely on the direction of the
afternoon breeze to protect your tent because mountain air currents usually, but not always, reverse in
the evening. A safe distance is usually twenty-five
or thirty feet unless you have a very strong evening
wind.

Everybody should help pitch each tent. One person should read the pitching directions, which are
included in most tents, while others string poles and
set stakes. This way everybody will know how each
shelter is set up, the party won't have to go through
the figuring out process again and pitching chores
can be divided.

Many backpacking books will tell you to dig a
shallow trench under your shoulders and hips. If you
are pitching on loose forest duff, it might be okay, although I don't think it adds much to the comfort. If
you have to actually excavate, the theoretical comfort will not compensate for the damage to the earth.
A lot has also been written about trenching around
the base of the tent, but if your shelter has a waterproof floor reaching above the sidewalls, and if you
haven't pitched in a gully, you won't need it. You
can also imagine what those rectangular earth-
works are going to look like after you leave.

If you are pitching in duff (that fine forest topsoil
composed of granulated bark, needles, and lightly

Setting Up Camp

decomposed branches), you are going to find getting
small skewer stakes to hold is a problem. There are
two ways of solving this problem: Replace the
original equipment skewers with channelized aluminum or plastic stakes, or weight down the skewers with rocks or branches. If you use rocks or
branches, be sure to replace them where you found
them when you break camp.

Be sure your shock-guys are tight and, before you
hit the sack, you might double-check them to make
sure they haven't loosened in cooler evening temperatures.

While you still have plenty of sunshine left, you
will want to unpack the sleeping bags and down
clothing to give them a chance to fluff out and dry.
Often perspiration seeps through to the backpack
and saturates a portion of the sleeping bag. A little
sun will dry it off and a breeze or shake once in a
while will have the compressed down billowing all
over the place. Drape the bags over convenient
bushes or small trees or rig up a clothesline from the
one-eighth-inch cord or the one-quarter-inch rope.
Make sure that wherever you put them they will
remain in the sun for awhile.

The final pre-dinner chore is to package the food
into one of the backpacks and suspend it off the
ground to keep the hungry and curious out of it.

Now everybody can tingle their toes in the icy
waters or find out what is biting in the lake.

Dinner

As evening begins to settle and the idea of coming
out of the cold water to the colder air becomes less
appealing, most hikers will begin to think about the
welfare of their stomachs. The spirit of cooperation

that governed the first shelter pitching will probably end here because, indeed, too many chefs do spoil the broth. Whoever ends up with the cooking chores, and they probably should be rotated from meal to meal, ought not have to do anything else. The rest of the party can gather the firewood, if you decide to build a fire in an already existing pit, establish a dishwashing responsibility, and see to other camp chores.

Sometime before the sun sets and the dew begins to settle, the sleeping bags, pads, and down clothing are going to have to be gathered and placed in their appropriate shelters. If any members of the party want to sleep out under the stars they are going to have to be reconciled to a lot of dew on their bags unless covers are provided. There are outdoor bag covers available called bivouac sacks which roughly sandwich the sleeping bag between a waterproof ground cloth and a water resistant but porous top. They are easy to make merely by sewing together appropriately cut-to-size pieces of these two fabrics.

A large poncho folded over the bag also makes a good cover and groundcloth provided the waterproof fold over the sack is staked out above so that body moisture will not soak back through the bag.

Outside sleepers should have reservations in one of the shelters because the romance of the stars is easily dampened by a nighttime storm.

A dinner fire should be just that, not a roaring blaze to singe the eyebrows of its beholders. It is assumed the firepit was inherited and, although it may not be picture-perfect, it will probably do, just the way it is. The hardest pits to cook out of are round because it is virtually impossible to avoid flames for delicate coal-cooking. If your secondhand pit is round, you can rearrange the rocks in a rectangular fashion so the fire and glowing coals can be segregated at opposite ends.

It goes without saying that green logs should be avoided. Not only are they hard to start and burn, not only do they require a saw or hatchet to cut, but they also kill the tree and maim the forest. In a well-used site, you may have to go far afield to find suitable fuel. Look for downed trees with projecting, air-dried limbs that can be broken off. Haul them back to camp whole and break them to size by stamping on them under leverage.

Often lakes and streams have a bonanza of bone-dry firewood in old snags and woodjams. Use it in moderation because these old carcasses are part of the charm of the wilderness.

If everything is soggy, use one of the fire-starting tablets to get the fire going then stack your stash of wood close to the fire to dry. Hard, dry wood burns incredibly hot and fast—thus all the concern about forest fires. You don't need or want a lot on the fire at any time; the blaze should be kept just barely adequate to boil water and should be fed only enough fuel to keep it at this level. As the first couple of generations of sticks are burned to coals, scrape them into the back of the pit where the finer points of the culinary arts can be performed. In the meantime, water boiling in pots suspended over the flames can be used for tea or coffee while the main course is cooking.

Unless you have a fresh fish or two—which are sinfully good slowly roasted over hot coals—water is probably about all you will need. Boil water over the fire for mixing dishes, and simmer it over the coals.

I usually have a soup every dinner and my own personal favorite is the packaged Top Ramen Chinese noodle soup which makes a nutritious and tasty

base for any number of dishes. I usually add powdered eggs and milk to the cold water before boiling
and often throw in some freeze-dried vegetables or
meats for variety. This personal staple is quick,
easy, light in the pack, and does not require a lot of
utensils or fooling around. It may not tingle the buds
in description but it is a hell of a lot better than my
boots and has amazed and delighted many backpacking companions.

I like powdered eggs and milk—they add both
taste and protein—in just about everything I cook
for trail dinners. An insipid package of powdered po-
tatoes can taste somewhat better than my boot with
the added flavor and texture of these light, simple
ingredients.

I am usually content with a second cup of tea and
a mug of cocoa for dessert but many people, especially kids, appreciate something with more body
such as instant pudding. Mix the pudding while the
water is boiling for the main course and let it cool in
the lake or stream. By dessert time it should be firm
and welcome.

Cooking is a very personal thing and you should
plan your meals around the minimum standards of
the party. If you don't think everybody is going to be
content with a thick soup, then better carry the
lightweight makings of a stew or a freeze-dried
casserole. But the boiled boot formula is valid, just
about anything tastes good with a fresh-air-and-
exercise whetted appetite. Don't aim too high on the
hog.

Cleanup

Cleanup should follow dinner closer than a yawn.
The longer dried- and caked-on foods remain on the

pots, the harder they are to get off. Scrape all remaining food into the fire and pick up any leavings around the dining area. This may be just insignificant garbage to you but it is steak to the woodland creatures who would be more than glad to start where you left off, invading your tranquil campsite in the middle of night.

Boil a large pot of water and pour in a cap of soap. Distribute the soapy water among all the dirty dishes and scour them completely. After returning the water to the main pot, check each dish carefully for any signs of leftover food. Everything spotless including the pot? Fine, dig a hole away from the river or lake and pour in the soapy water. Then refill the pot and rinse off the dishes, pouring that water into the hole too. When you are sure you have all the soap off, rinse everything again in the open water and stack the dishes face down to drain and dry. Might as well leave the hole open until after the morning's dishes have been cleaned.

Securing the camp for night is a matter of making sure no food, either scraps or supplies, is going to be available to after-dinner guests. Tightly enclose the larder in one of the small backpacks (so it will be waterproof), and string it between two trees or suspend it from a high branch.

Make sure that anything you don't want wet, which probably should include the rest of the packs, is under cover, either inside under tents, or under a poncho. Everything you need for the night—sleeping bags, pads, stuff sacks, sweaters and jackets for pillows, water, aspirin, and night clothes—should be handy inside the tents or under shelters.

All clear? Good, now you can relax and enjoy the sunset and the first magic moments of the night until the exertions of the day and the dampening cold send you staggering to bed.

Sleeping

Getting a good night's sleep is one of those bodily functions, like moving the bowels, which the mind cannot seem to entirely control or regulate. Most people when traveling have a tough time falling off in a strange bed listening to strange sounds with a strange sense of place.

And most hikers, even hard-core veterans, have an immensely difficult time getting soundly to sleep on the first night out. The traveling phenomenon is compounded in camping by the knowledge that just a thin coat of nylon is between you and a mysterious nighttime world that is strange and perhaps a little frightening. You are alert to every minor sound out of place—a cracked twig or the soft rustling of needles. These sounds, which at home would probably not penetrate the consciousness, seem to demand a response in the wilds. Consequently, every time you are drifting into a sound sleep, something jars you out of it.

Added to this creeping-creature syndrome are some physiological problems. It is virtually impossible to be as comfortable in a tent as at home. A half-inch-thick Ensolite pad isn't the cloud nine mattress in the bedroom and it is hard to sprawl in a mummy bag (although there are tricks that you will learn). You are wearier than you have been in a long time and may have reached that point of "sleepless sleepiness." There is a pain in your toe, your knee aches, and every muscle in your body feels like it is sprung. On top of that, your feet are so hot they are sweating but your legs feel like they are caked in ice. And you know that if you don't get a good night's sleep tonight, you are going to be under great stress and fall off a cliff tomorrow.

And the odd thing is that all of these nagging fears, anxieties, aches, and discomforts will disappear the second night. You won't be as tired as you feared during the day, and the second night out you sleep like a baby. The sounds float over you unnoticed, the sleeping bag and pad actually do feel like your cloud nine, the aches and pains soothe themselves and there is no thought about tomorrow because the trails all lead downhill.

I have the curse too. Even if I was hiking the week before, I still bounce around the first night, knowing full well that the things that are harassing me tonight won't mean a thing tomorrow night. But I am never especially tired the day after what was apparently a completely restless night and I have come to the conclusion that we actually sleep better than we think while we are tossing around in the tent. I think the wakeful interludes between starts from a half-sleep are evidently not as long as they seem and we spend most of the first night in a half-sleep torpor.

A friend of mine says she crawls into her bag the first night knowing she isn't going to get a wink. She says there is a joyful anticipation of listening to the sounds of the night and watching the stars. She doesn't plan to do much the second day so nothing will really be lost and a lot of new experience will be gained.

However, she adds, she is often staring off into the heavens when her eyes begin to nod, and she opens them again to the sun crawling over the eastern peaks. Anxiety about sleep is probably the real prob-

lem and if you are able to convince yourself that you
are indifferent, nature will probably take its course.

Sleep will be less elusive if you are as comfortable
as possible. Fluff out your bag well before crawling
in. Make sure your pad covers both your hips and
shoulders. If there is a bad lump or sharp object coming through, move around to see if it can be avoided.
If not, go outside and dig around under the tent until
you are satisfied. Pillows add a lot of comfort and security so take the time to make yours as fluffy as you
can. The insulation of your bag can be regulated to
some degree by adjusting the zipper. Some bags, in
fact, come with zippers that adjust from both the top
and the bottom. If it is an unusually warm night,
just start the zipper and leave the rest of it open. As
it cools, zip to comfort.

Striking Camp

Your face may look like a topographical map by
morning but it really wasn't bad, was it? Besides,
you don't have far to go for your next camp so take
your time getting up, scratching around, and getting
breakfast.

The bags should be hung on the line as soon as
you are out of them. Anything else that got wet
overnight should be moved into the sun to dry before
packing.

Stoves are much better for cooking breakfast than
fires. The glow that was so cozy last night will be uncomfortably warm this morning in the gaining heat.
Also, the fire is going to have to be completely out
and the pit cleaned before you leave which will
mean a great deal of extra bother after the meal is
cooked. It may take a little longer to cook an enjoy-
able breakfast on a single-burner stove (although

not much, because stoves concentrate heat better than fires), but remember you are in no hurry.

My favorite breakfast, perhaps because I am more indolent than epicurean, is a healthful bowl of oatmeal and peanut butter. It not only fills me up sufficiently but also, as we discussed earlier, tends to make me overfull. I would personally prefer to keep food moving through my system than attempt that unforgettable trailside breakfast that nobody will remember by noon.

Oatmeal also has the advantage of cooking quickly and cleanly. Regular oatmeal requires only a three- to five-minute simmer, and instant oatmeal puffs up with boiling water. Top off your oatmeal with a cup of coffee and you are ready to hike or trot.

Breaking camp should be done in more or less the reverse order of pitching. With breakfast dishes washed and drying with the final dishwater poured into the drain hole and it covered and looking like part of the forest, start folding and packing the gear. Try not to pack anything wet because the moisture will surely get around the pack. Now would be a good time to experiment with pack sizes and weights to see if some of the smaller members are capable of carrying more than yesterday.

Repack the tent with the thought in mind of protecting the floor and fly from rubbing and punctures. Most good tents come with a pole bag. Collapse and fit the poles together, then poke the stakes into the open holes of one side of the stack. Put them all in the bag with the stakes down. I usually fold the fly separately and lay it on top of the unfolded tent canopy. Then fold the canopy down so that it will surround the bottom and roll the whole up into a cylinder with the fly in the middle. The tent goes into the stuff bag first, then jam the pole bag down, bottom (or stake end), first.

Now that the bags are packed, police the camping site for anything you might have left behind, wanted or unwanted. Pack the undegradable trash in one of your empty dinner plastic bags along with any leavings from previous visitors.

Dig the ash out of the firepit and spread it lightly around. Some say you should also dismantle the fireplace and redistribute the rocks but that is ethically an open question and up to each party. It is most certainly your ethical responsibility to see that everything else is clean and as close to its natural condition as possible. If your party leaves the campsite as clean as found or cleaner, the odds of sleeping well the second night are vastly improved; at least you will have a clear conscience.

The second day's hike and your second camp will more or less follow the rules of the first day. However, there are a few differences in procedure for the downhill-home trek. The most critical difference is pace.

Downhill hiking is, obviously, much less tiring than uphill but it is also more wearing on the joints and dangerous. Every step is dropping an awful lot of energy on ankles, knees, and hips. Keep the stride about the same as on the uphill leg. The pace will be quicker because you won't need nearly as many breathing stops. Also, everybody should really lean on their bootlaces for the downhill pull because the feet have a tendency to slam forward with each step and push toes into the front of the boot. If somebody starts complaining about sore toes, stop immediately and tighten up the laces. If you have a bad knee or weak ankle, you might take the precaution of wrapping it with a pressure bandage before starting.

If you had some hard pitches on the way up, they will be harder on the way down. If somebody feels insecure, rope up as you did on the way up and impress on everybody the preeminent importance of footholds over handholds. (Footholds are much harder to see when going down.) Take your time and retreat with style—you are being judged on grace rather than speed.

Kids seem to have an irresistible urge to run the last quarter-mile, but remember the dignity of the party—and loose rocks—and keep the pace even. There, that wasn't so bad was it?

There are things that make backpack hiking a really soul-soaring experience.

CHAPTER TEN

Appreciation and Ethics

There is nothing anybody can say that is going to make you appreciate backpacking and the new look at the world you get from the perspective of high ground gained on your own two feet. Books can lure you onto the trail with promises of rebirth or transcendental experiences in the wilds, but there are no books that can put you up there a second time if the first trip was not worthwhile.

Almost everybody knows that backpacking is more work than golf, and they are prepared to sweat a little on the first trip. Just about everybody is also prepared for a feeling that they have stepped out of the real world of machines and instant communications into an unfamiliar nether world of sublime gentleness and fury. But most people cannot really bolster themselves for the stark and sometimes alarming feeling of naked isolation. It begins to nibble at the stomach the moment you step away from the trailhead and swells as the distance grows. For most people it will manifest itself as a flight of the heart, a feeling that something long lost has finally been regained.

For others it will be a fluttering of the heart increasing hourly with the anxieties and physical discomforts. And there are still others who will regard it as a sheer bore and an intolerable waste of energy and time.

Weather can have an awful lot to do with the legacies of the first trip. Fine, bright days that are not too warm, fostering a sense of well-being in a strange land, are easy to take, and just about anybody can come away with a profit from the trip. But most trips, even short ones, are not going to be all blue skies and soft breezes. A day or two of dismal drizzle or blisters on top of aching feet will soon invoke a mound of resentment.

Assuming, however, the first try was a success and you already have your gear, you may as well plan more trips in a variety of areas. Each wild area has its distinct character that can make sampling them all a delight. Eventually you will want to expand the distance of the hike and the amount of time adrift in the wilderness.

There seems to be a ratio of decivilization proportionate to the number of days you spend in the wilds. The first one, two, or three days you are a civilized being stumbling awkwardly through the pristine world of nature. Then, without any conscious awareness, your attitude begins to change. Everything about you in the hills becomes familiar and the thoughts of life below become hazier and less beguiling. You and your equipment become functional members of the wilderness community and by the end of a week or so on the country, the thought of returning to civilization becomes a somewhat frightening trauma. I speak in all seriousness—this happens to just about everybody with a yearning for the wilderness.

Born hikers are naturally climbers and most of them will try a summit sometime and mountaineering, no pun intended, is the highest form of backpacking expression.

While you are seeking bigger and better backpacking challenges, don't drag reluctant hikers in your steps. If the attrition of one or two hikes has left members of your family with something better to do, let them do it. If you and your spouse are the only ones left when the dust of your first hike has settled, fine. The relationship of long-married couples can be retempered by regular baptisms in the hills. Or the bonds between one parent and a child or two can also be cemented by the thick and thin of the wilderness.

You may even have to look around for an entirely new set of backpacking chums, but this is alright too, because someplace out there is a person or two who may want exactly the same thing out of the wilderness as you.

THE COMMUNITY

The higher you go and the farther afield you travel, the more aware you will become of the structure of the wilderness. You will notice that hills do not have the same texture or construction as the mountains above them. You will also discover that the nature of the forest and vegetation changes from area to area and at different altitudes. As the forest ecology changes, so does the animal community within that forest. You will soon want to know what these species are and what separates them. You will be curious to know whether the geological formation you are hiking in was created by glaciers or is composed of an ancient volcanic eruption. There is usually abundant information available on geology and wildlife from the agency that controls the area or from a state university.

Most state and national parks also have booklets or pamphlets on the nature of their lands. You can usually send for these ahead of time by inquiring with the park superintendent's office.

This doesn't of course, mean that you are going to have to burn the midnight oil at home studying the literature about your next backpack objective, but at some point you are going to want to know whether you are clambering over igneous or sedimentary rock and when you are in the aeolian zone of a mountain. You will wonder what the delicate little pink flowers on the bristly dark green bushes are and why they grow at 8,000 feet.

Animals

You will also find that knowing the difference between a hairy marmot and a badger will put you on different terms with these animals. Bears, as awesome as they are, melt into the animal community after you know what they eat, when they hibernate, and how long they live.

The white-tailed deer you saw nibbling grass by the streamside was charming enough by itself but even more compelling if you knew why it was eating grass rather than browsing the willows which are its normal fare.

Trees change radically as you ascend a hill. Along a stream, the lower ones will probably be leafy deciduous trees which will evolve into cedars, and finally peter out into occasional spruce or fir. You can almost measure your climb by observing the trees along the trail.

Birds

Birds are another part of the wilderness that should be understood to be thoroughly enjoyed. Just about everybody can recognize the majestic soar of an eagle but do you know what that large, gray, squawking bird is that keeps following you up the trail? In the west, there is a small water bird called a dipper (or water ouzel), which seems to relish keeping hikers company by the streamside. It bobs around from rock to rock dipping its fanny in a preposterous bow and will occasionally entertain you with its mystifying feat of walking underwater from one rock to another.

Much of the northeast highland area is graced with occasional visits from cedar waxwings which also seem to enjoy regaling hikers with their splendor from a trailside bush.

Fishing

Remote or alpine lake fishing is a good way of whiling away the camp hours and adding fresh protein to the dinner meal. In mountain country, these fish will be mostly trout—native brook trout in the East, and variations of the cutthroat trout in the West. In the flatlands, you can find some really exciting bass and pike fishing in out-of-the-way lakes.

Most wilderness fish are wild—that is they grew up there and often they are the descendants of the fish that originally populated these lakes. They are wild by virtue of original stocks being left ample enough in waters sufficiently pristine to generate while their cousins in lower waters have been starved, poisoned, or "caught out." These wild-stocked hinterland lakes should be considered sacred monuments and their denizens should be killed only with a full awareness of their value.

Fish in these backcountry lakes, especially above the timberline, are extremely vulnerable. They have only an instant each year to eat enough food to actually grow. The temperate season in the alpine region is often less than two months long, leaving these fish another ten months of slim pickings and fat-resorbing torpor. It takes an alpine cutthroat four years to reach sexual maturity, and at maturity they sometimes never exceed six or seven inches in length.

Needless to say, during the short harvest season they are extremely hungry and willing to try just about anything that remotely resembles food. It takes very little skill and absolutely no brains to haul a flopping string of these rare and valuable creatures into camp. And the pity of it is most of them are usually left in a heap for whatever scavenging animal might come along (and this could easily be a bear in the middle of the night who will want a lot more than your fish for his trouble). Gauge your catch by what can be moderately eaten at the next meal.

Bait fishing is not recommended, if not on legal grounds (it is forbidden in many national park waters), then on ethical and practical grounds. In the first place, it is hard to find native bait at timberline elevations. The same rule that applies to austere existence of the fish will also hold for filling

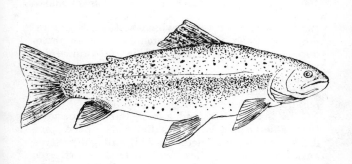

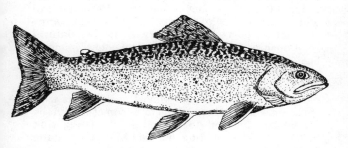

J.B. SANDOVAL

Wilderness Trout

Top: The cutthroat trout has a distinctive red slash under the throat and dark spots against a light background. *Bottom:* The brook trout is actually a charr with light spots against a dark olive background.

the bait tin. Importing lowland baits such as min-
nows is totally unconscionable because an introduced species could take hold in the thin alpine
water and wipe out the natives. Once a fish is
hooked on bait it is almost impossible to release it
unharmed because of the damage normally done by
bait hooks to the gullet or gills.

This leaves flies and lures. Lures, especially
the treble-hooked variety, suffer some of the same
drawbacks as bait (including being illegal in some
backwater lakes). They tend to hook a little too
easily and let go a little too hard to be sure a
released fish will survive. Also there is a matter of
aesthetics. You got all the way up to the lake
without the advantage of gears and turning wheels,
and your life for the next couple of days will be
reduced to a one-to-one mechanical ratio on the trail
and in camp, so why add the complication of whir-
ring metal parts to an otherwise honest natural
relationship? Spinning reels belong below, in motor
boats and among automobiles, but they are definitely out of place in the wilderness.

Which leaves flies and fly tackle. You can catch
too many fish on a flyrod almost as easily as with
bait or spoon but there seems to be something in the
simple commitment to motion in flycasting that
makes the living motion of a humiliated but living
trout swimming away from your hands more pleas-
ing than the burden of your creel. Fly fishermen normally can't cover an entire body of water as easily as
spin fishermen because of the limitation of the back
cast. But there is usually an opening in the trees or a
gap in the facing wall that permits a good backcast
and, if the fish are feeding, a flycaster has as good a
chance of catching one for dinner as a bait or lure
fisherman.

An eight-foot rod with a relatively delicate line (say a five or six weight), will drop a dry fly nicely or propel a streamer or nymph far enough. Wilderness fish are not the scholars sometimes found below and brightness in the fly should do the trick. The points on your leaders need not be as fine; alpine trout don't seem to mind strings attached to their manna.

Swimming

In alpine mountain waters, about the only consideration in taking a dip is the temperature of the water. This is assuming the air is warm enough to make the prospect of a swim inviting. Water temperature seldom gets above fifty in high lakes and streams and often stays in the forties all summer long. In other words, stick your foot in before taking a dive.

Some lowland backwaters can be seething with leeches or lampreys and if you go far enough in the Deep South it is possible to find cottonmouths.

Side Trips

Wilderness trails usually follow the path of least resistance to a given destination. This means they often avoid some really interesting places and spectacular views. Your map, which by now has taken on a three-dimensional quality, should give you an idea of what's around and how to get there. Side trips from the trail will add a bit of glamour to your first couple of hikes and the experience of setting off across the trackless bush can develop into cross-country hikes in the future. Remember, however, to always direction-orient your map before leaving the trail and take and hold accurate bearings.

Your first few side trips should be modest treks, no more than, say, a couple of miles from the trail or camp. When you get your off-trail footing and bearings down, you can wander farther afield. When you do finally decide to make a cross-country overnight, remember that the rules of camping and firebuilding have changed. The legacy of your off-trail trip should be nothing: No scraps of paper, no broken branches, no visible trail, and especially no visible camping site. The tracks you leave in the mud will wash away soon and your passing will be no better marked than the ranging of a bear. You will truly be a part of the wilderness community.

AND NOW, A WORD ABOUT OUR PRODUCT

This element in our American landscape which you will come to see as the last stand of truth and beauty, is being looked at by others in quite a different perspective. These small and ever-eroding bastions of wilderness escaped the march of civilization across the continent only because they were too poor in marketable natural resources or too inaccessible to make exploitation worthwhile.

However, as markets for natural resources swell and supplies in already developed areas diminish, attention is focused on those small enclaves of remote materials passed by on the first sweep. The resource exploiters begin to lobby, angle, and squirm for the privilege of chopping, digging, or paving these humble monuments to what was and what should be.

If you think these greedy, single-minded, and unphilosophical Philistines want to tear the heart and guts out of the wilderness to satisfy some psychotic lust, you are dead wrong. They do it because you and I, and just about everybody else in this country, encourage them to do it.

We use more of everything than any other nation in the history of the world has ever used. We use ten times the amount of water every day than any other people in the world use and when the Philistines want to dam a stream in a wild area they are doing it so that we can use eleven times as much water as we really need. We use enough petroleum every day, in our cars and plastic trinkets, to choke us, and the exploiters are always looking for more to speed up our suicidal asphyxiation. Just about everything we did in the past utilizing our minds and muscles—from communicating to brushing our teeth—we now do with electricity. And the substandard coal in our hills and prairies will be scraped out to keep us electrified until our hair stands on end.

We elect our policymakers on promises of "economic growth" and "a larger slice in the world economic pie," then let them wheel-and-deal away our wild lands to make us richer and sadder.

And we eat. Boy, do we eat. We eat so much we can't even get it all down. The average American family throws away enough food every day to feed families in underdeveloped nations for a week. Our rivers are running foul with the waste by-products of our appetites and the agribusiness folks are more than happy to chemically fertilize a little more wild marginal cropland to sate our bloated bodies.

Even though you and I aren't the ones who are dismantling our wilderness heritage, these areas are being desecrated in our behalf. We consume the blood and bone of the wilderness then pick our teeth, burp, and lament its passing. Ultimately, the enemy is us.

This backpacking business may seem to be getting out of hand. First of all you are expected to spend the family fortune on a bunch of equipment (much of which is made from petroleum products), then carry all that stuff sweating and grunting up a hill, survive days and nights of real and imagined terrors, and now you are asked to feel guilty for living the way everybody else lives. It is true that appreciation of the wilderness is going to make demands on your everyday life. And when you come to really transcend those metaphysical barriers between civilization and wilderness—that feeling of belonging that comes with a few days out—then the sacrifices won't be so demanding.

You will not regret turning off the television, burning only the lights you need, working in a cooler but healthier winter temperature, buying only what you really need, preparing and eating only what you can easily digest, driving to work or shopping with others or walking rather than driving, and voting for people who are committed to resource conservation.

You will find that most of these austerity measures come naturally. You won't want a new chrome-plated car every other year, nor a new house every ten. The absurdity of disposable containers and all-but-disposable gadgets will become second nature. And you will eat less but better knowing that plastic or chemically grown food is neither good for you nor good for the world. You will be healthier because you won't be relying on nature's purloined energy to do all your work for you. And, of course, you will be happier—closer to your family and friends than you ever were because your lives have taken on a new direction.

When you reach this magic transitional stage

between wilderness and civilization, you will become more conscious of what is happening not only to wild lands but also the whole environment. You will discover that there are a lot of others around who feel the same way and want parts of the landscape left as they are. You will find that together, you and others can justify alternative values for wilderness and natural resources; that you can make politicians and land managers see that a tree can be a tree rather than a few disposable tablecloths; that wilderness land on top of coal or metals has greater value than the volts or votes the resources would produce; that others don't have to cluster posh ghettos in the hills to enjoy these lands; and that leaders can no longer lead if they don't listen to the people.

Name Dropping: Equipment Recommendations

Trying to sift through the various equipment labels these days is almost like random selection of a card from a deck. There is an unbelievable assortment of firms, both large and small, making an unimaginable array of backpacking equipment.

To make the process of selecting gear easier and a bit less arbitrary, here is a list of the necessary items and a few firms that I have found to offer either adequate equipment at a modest price or exceptional quality gear at a commensurate price. This list is not nearly complete (indeed, there are virtually hundreds of different options), and there are probably many makers of fine, reasonably priced equipment that have been left out. But I have examined or used items from all of the firms noted and feel that design, workmanship, and price make them reasonably good choices.

Most manufacturers make more than one item—for instance, both sleeping bags and tents—but addresses and general comments will be restricted to only one equipment category.

Boots

Fabiano. Dept. A-9, 850 Summer Street, South Boston, Massachusetts 02127. A fine boot at a reasonable price. They are one of the few European makers who fit wide feet; most shops and mail order houses carry their large line.

Pivetta. Donner Mountain Corporation, Berkeley, California. An interesting and well-designed line with inside lightweight stitching on welts even into heavier duty boots; another European firm that caters to wide feet.

Danner. Dept. B, P.O. Box 22204, Portland, Oregon 97222. A carefully made American boot priced about the same as better European boots. Both their hiking and mountaineering boots are available in wider sizes.

Tecnica. Dartmouth Outdoor Sports, Hanover, New Hampshire 03755. A likeable boot in a well-thought-out line of weights and functions. Enough sizes to fit anybody, and at a reasonable price.

Galibier. Mountain Paraphernalia, Box 4536, Modesto, California 95352.

Vasque. P.O. Box 25715, Salt Lake City, Utah 84125. Making boots under their own and several other labels, Vasques are good quality and relatively inexpensive. Like most American-made boots, Vasque can fit just about anyone in both size and function.

Lowa. 1234 5th Street, Dept. BPW, Berkeley, California 94710. Extremely strong, tough mountaineering boots.

Raichle. Molitor USA, Natic, Massachusetts 01760. An average boot at an average price.

Herman Shoe Company. Dept. 34, Millis, Massachusetts 02054. The "Survivor" is a popular boot at a good price. It is a medium-weight, high-top boot to be had in all sizes.

Sleeping Bags

Camp 7. 802 South Sherman, Longmont, Colorado 80501. Camp 7 specializes in very fine bags for all purposes and all sizes. Prices moderate to high.

Slumberjack. Los Angeles, California. A good line of down and synthetic bags of fair quality at modest prices.

Sierra Designs. 4th and Addison Streets, Berkeley, California 94710. Exceptionally high quality bags and other soft gear.

Holubar Mountaineering. P.O. Box 7, Boulder, Colorado 80302. A large line of ingeniously designed and carefully crafted synthetic and down bags for people willing to spend the money.

Paul Petzoldt Wilderness Equipment. Box 78, Lander, Wyoming 82520. Pioneers in spartan mountaineering synthetic-filled bags. They are reasonably priced but available only by mail.

Hirsch-Weis. 5203 S.E. Johnson Creek Boulevard, Portland, Oregon 97206. Modest quality at a modest price. Widely available through sporting goods stores.

Class 5. 2010 Seventh Street, Berkeley, California 94710. A small firm that makes generally fine equipment at a price that shouldn't make you lose sleep. Their "Nickel Cigar" down bag comes in one size and if you fit, it is a good buy.

Snow Lion. P.O. Box 9056, Berkeley, California, 94709. Exceptionally fine quality down and synthetic bags in many styles, shapes, and sizes. You pay for what you get.

The North Face. Dept. BP-2, 1234 Fifth Street, Berkeley, California 94710. Another well-respected firm offering an outstanding line of down and synthetic bags at fair prices.

Alpine Designs. 6185 Arapahoe, Boulder, Colorado 80303. Make a clever strip-baffled synthetic bag as well as a full line of down sleepers.

Ascente. 2126 Inyo Street, Fresno, California 93718. An old, established equipment maker offering a current line of bags including both down and Fibrefill II synthetic insulation.

Backpacks

Kelty. 9281 Borden Avenue, Sun Valley, California 91352. Was in the vanguard of the postwar backpacking renaissance, and the Kelty frame is still regarded by many as the standard.

Camp Trails. 4111 Clarendon Avenue, Phoenix, Arizona 85019. Has been around nearly as long as Kelty with less elaborate and more moderately priced frame packs.

Jansport. Paine Field Industrial Park, Everett, Washington 98204. Making a full line of slightly iconoclastic equipment including elegant frame packs, modest frames, and a long line of internal frames and daypacks. They also offer one of the many recent variations on the weight-bearing, self-frame soft packs (although theirs has a set of padded internal stays).

Gerry. 5450 North Valley Highway, Denver, Colorado 80216. Another established firm making a full line of backpacking gear. Their packs range from a heavy-duty frame pack to light daypacks and include a lovely variation on the weight-bearing soft pack design.

Trailwise. 2407 Fourth Street, Berkeley, California 94710. A newer firm making a complete backpacking line. They offer several different frame pack models as well as a number of simple daypacks.

Maran. Northwest Wilderness Travel, 8705 Twenty-fifth Street, N.E., Seattle, Washington 98115. Introduced handlebars on external frames several years ago, enabling backpackers to relieve their shoulders by hoisting packs from the bottom. They also have a large line of soft daypacks.

Cannondale. 35 Pulaski Street, Stamford, Connecticut 06902. This company makes a stout, internally framed pack and several daypack designs.

Wilderness Experience. 9421 Winnetka Avenue, Chatsworth, California 91311. A new firm making only packs, from those having stout frames to tiny bicycle bags. As pack specialists, they seem to be able to offer very neatly designed and made packs at reasonable prices.

Hine. Box 4059, Boulder, Colorado 80302. Another newcomer specializing in packs and offering a nifty dozen, from a tough internally framed model to small hiker sacks.

Alpine Designs. (See Sleeping Bags for address.) A substantial line of frame and unframed softpacks.

The North Face. (See Sleeping Bags for address.) A few proven internally framed packs and soft daysacks.

Sierra Designs. (See Sleeping Bags for address.) A line of well-thought-out packs from frames to daypacks.

Mountain Equipment. 3208 Hamilton, Fresno, California 93702. A new company making good packs, from large to small.

The Great Pacific Iron Works. Box 150, Ventura, California 93001. Primarily interested in mountaineering hardware. They do, however, make several packs including a remarkably fine (and expensive), weight-bearing softpack.

Rivendell Mountain Works. Box 198, Victor, Idaho 83455. This firm makes a relatively narrow line of extremely fine mountaineering gear, starting with the Jensen pack which was the first (and may still be the best), of the weight-bearing softpacks.

Alpenlite. Box 851, Claremont, California 91711. Their popular and well-conceived, hip-hugging frame is available in a variety of sack combinations at a reasonable price.

Tents

More than any other piece of basic equipment, tents have a baffling spread in price and quality. You can buy a suitable two-man tent with a fly for $75, or spend up to $225 for a lavish two-man mountain tent. Although there are several inexpensive tents that will do nicely for temperate weather backpacking, you really can't spend too much on a good tent. The more you pay, the better your tent will be and the longer it will last.

Stephenson. RFD 4, Box 389, Gilford, New Hampshire 03246. The tents are called "Warm-lites," and light they are. Models range from five to two pounds. But you pay dearly for the lightweight special materials, clever dome designs, and meticulous workmanship.

Jansport. (See Backpacks for address.) Makes one of the few other lines of dome tents with a series of two- to six-person, self-supporting half-globes. They are a bit cheaper than Stephensons but a lot heavier.

Eureka Tent Company. Box 966, Binghamton, New York 13902. Make perhaps the most accessible and best inexpensive tent on the market. Their A-frame models range from $75 to $110 and suit most needs. Their famous "Draw-tite" line—a semi-dome—is a bit costlier and heavier but still highly regarded by many veterans.

Gerry. (See Backpacks for address.) A company that has been making some of the best reasonably priced tents on the market for some time. They are a tad heavier than some, but wear like iron.

Camp Trails. (See Backpacks for address.) They offer an inexpensive line of tents covering most fair weather needs.

Rivendell Mountain Works. (See Backpacks for address.) This manufacturer offers one very expensive two-man tent for a relatively limited purpose. It is an extremely well-designed, high altitude, crush-proof affair that probably does not belong in a hiker's backpack.

Camp-Ways. 12915 South Spring Street, Los Angeles, California 90061. This firm offers a reasonably well made and designed line of imported tents that should fit most budgets. Better models have breathable tops and flies and are satisfactory for most three-season uses.

Caribou Mountaineering. 174 East 8th Avenue, Chico, California 95926. A new firm making sophisticated mountaineering tents at somewhat less than you would expect to pay.

Mountain Safety Research. 631 South 96th Street, Seattle, Washington 98108. MSR makes some of the best thought-out equipment available. You can buy simple summer A-frames or domes for under $100 or pay well over $200 for elegant mountaineering tents. Either way, you will probably get your money's worth.

The North Face. (See Sleeping Bags for address.) Famous high-quality tents ranging from simple lowland models to strong expedition shelters.

Sierra Designs. (See Sleeping Bags for address.) Another firm with a good reputation for a finely made, tough line of tents.

Alpine Designs. (See Sleeping Bags for address.) This company offers several sizes and functions of fairly expensive tents.

Trailwise. (See Backpacks for address.) A sensible line of tents including the famous Fitzroy series mountain shelters. Prices are about average for higher quality tents.

Holubar Mountaineering. (See Sleeping Bags for address.) This firm offers an extremely fine but relatively expensive line of tents ranging from a light two-man to an elegant four-person tent.

Hirsch-Weis. (See Sleeping Bags for address.) Stag tents are fairly inexpensive and easily available. They offer a number of attractively priced, waterproof-topped tents, but you are better off spending a little extra for a porous top and a fly.

Weatherproofs

There is so little variation in the design of ponchos, cagoules, and rain jackets that it is hardly worthwhile to generally analyze competitive products. Most companies that make sleeping bags, packs, or tents also make a poncho, and several make cagoules or rain jackets. The general comments on price and quality of a manufacturer's other gear should give you an idea of what to expect in their weatherproofs.

Clothing

In just about all the varied forms of backpacking, clothing means wool and down- or synthetic-insulated garments. Everyday wool sweaters, shirts, and slacks will do, and may have to do, because there are few suppliers of wool backpacking garments in the United States.

Woolrich. Woolrich, Pennsylvania 17779. By far the largest of the outdoor apparel manufacturers is Woolrich, which makes wool and down clothing to cover you from head to foot. Their wool shirts, sweaters, knickers, and pants are excellent quality but fairly expensive. Their down clothing, including jackets and vests, are good quality at a lower than average price.

Wigwam Mills. Sheboygan, Wisconsin 53081. One of the few U.S. makers of good ragg socks. Their wool-blend ragg is about the most comfortable and longlasting I have found and costs about the same as others.

Pendleton Mills. Pendleton, Oregon 97801. Pendleton makes luxurious wool shirts and pants, at luxury prices.

L. L. Bean. 278 Maine St., Freeport, Maine 04032. Mostly known as an outfitter, Bean makes extremely high-quality wool pants and shirts that will wear long after you have forgotten the price.

Down-Insulated Clothing

Down clothing is a bit easier to locate. Nearly all makers of tents, packs, and sleeping bags also have lightweight down or synthetic garments. Most backpacking or mountaineering shops carry more than one line of down clothing and most sporting goods or discount stores have less expensive and slightly less suitable lines.

Eddie Bauer, P.O. Box 3700, Seattle, Washington 98124. Certainly theirs is about the best-known, highest quality, and most expensive line of down clothing available. Although they also make sleeping bags, tents, and packs, Bauer is most famous for outdoor and backpacking attire which is available only through the mail or in one of their factory shops.

Compasses

Buying a compass is an easy choice because only two firms make good transparent-based azimuth compasses. There are several other brands on the market but none offer the quality and simplicity of operation.

Precise Imports Corp. 3 Chestnut Street, Suffern, New York 10901. Importers of the Finnish-made Suunto compass line which includes several price variations of the transparent-base compass.

Silva. 2466 N. St., Rd. 39, La Porte, Indiana 46350. Makers of the first, and probably most popular, transparent-based compass. Price range is identical with Suunto starting at about $5.

Sew-It-Yourself Aids

Most basic equipment items are available in kit form for people with enough sewing skill and patience to stitch them together. Most firms that offer kits have a full range including tents, sleeping bags, waterproofs, and down clothing. The savings are not great—from about one-fourth to one-third less than the price of a comparable readymade but in some cases this may be enough to get some people started in backpacking.

If you'd like to save more money than kits make possible, try making your own outdoor equipment from scratch. You can do it with the help of a very practical book, *Outdoor Gear You Can Make Yourself* by Marcia and Bob Lamoreaux. Not only does it contain easy-to-understand, step-by-step instructions for making tents, sleeping bags, rucksacks and many other useful items, it offers handy pointers on basic sewing techniques and shopping for a sewing machine.

Among the reliable companies supplying kits are the following:

Frostline. Department C, 452 Burbank, Broomfield, Colorado 80020.

Plain Brown Wrapper, Inc., 2055 West Amherst Ave., Englewood, Colorado 80110.

Altra Inc. 3645 Pearl Street, Boulder, Colorado 80301.

Holubar Mountaineering (see Sleeping Bags for address).

Eastern Mountain Sports. 1041 Commonwealth Ave., Boston, Massachusetts 02215.

Mail Order Shops

If at all possible, backpackers should do most of their buying personally from local mountaineering shops. This is especially critical in the case of boots where individual foot characteristics require precise fitting.

It isn't always possible, however, to get to a mountaineering shop, and there are several conscientious mail order stores that try hard to please and will accept undamaged returns. I have found all of the following firms carry excellent equipment and try to take good care of their mail order customers.

L. L. Bean. (See Clothing for address.) One of the oldest and most respected outfitters in the nation, Bean's handle a lot of backpacking equipment although they are primarily interested in outdoor sporting gear.

The Co-op Wilderness Supply. 1432 University Ave., Berkeley, California 94703. Their catalogue lists several products of good makers as well as less expensive items under their own label.

Sierra Designs. (See Sleeping Bags for address.) Catalogue includes a full line of backpacking gear featuring their own but also offering options by other makers as well.

Eastern Mountain Sports. (See Sew-It-Yourself Aids for address.) Catalogue lists equipment by most good manufacturers in addition to their own less expensive lines.

Eddie Bauer. (See Down-insulated Clothing for address.) Another well-known outfitter. Catalogue contains their own products as well as several items from other makers.

Kelty. (See Backpacks for address.) This firm offers a large catalogue containing Kelty packs and other house equipment as well as gear from other good manufacturers.

APPENDIX TWO

What You Should Know Before Setting Out

SITE SELECTION

After locating a suitable hiking area, check with state fish and game, conservation department or county surveyor to find out how much contiguous wild land there is in the area.

MAPS

Generally a managing agency such as the U.S. Forest Service, state forest department, U.S. Park Service, or U.S. Bureau of Land Management, will have road and trail maps of the area. You will also want a topographical map, often available at local sporting goods shops or they may be ordered from the U.S. Geological Survey in Denver, Colorado, 80225, (for maps west of the Rockies), and Washington, D.C. 20242 (for maps east of the Rockies).

You can find appropriate description of quadrant topographical maps from the county surveyor or the land management agency.

CONDITION OF TRAIL

Check with land management agencies, local sporting goods stores, or the state department of fish and game for trail obstructions, possible difficult areas (cliffs, creeks, swamps, or snowfields), and the general condition of the trail. Also see if you can discover how much time is required to reach a certain overnight objective, such as a lake.

SUITABILITY OF CAMPSITE

Sporting goods stores or the state fish and game department should be able to tell you about the fish and fishing or swimming in lakes or streams along the trail.

HEALTH AND SAFETY CONDITIONS

Check with the land management authority or state fish and game about the safety of the drinking water. They should also know what you can expect in mosquitoes or other insect pests, poisonous plants or snakes, and other problem animals. Also check fire regulations.

EMERGENCY HELP

Check with the county sheriff about a search and rescue squad or volunteer deputy rescue posse. Find out where the nearest accessible phone is to your trail and the emergency number of the rescue

agency. Write it down and give each member of the
party a copy. Also check your map and consult a
land management agency about the easiest and
quickest overland route out of the area. This should
intersect a road running at right angles to the overland direction—such as a north-south road running
along the eastern boundary of your backpacking
area which can be reached with a general easterly
bearing from the trail.

TRANSPORTATION

If you intend to leave your car in town, you will
have to know if a bus service can conveniently leave
you off and pick you up near the trailhead. Or, you
may want to make previous arrangements with a
friend or gas station attendant to provide trans-
portation.

LEAVING WORD

Give a copy or drawing of a map (with your
proposed route sketched in and the time you anticipate returning), to a friend or relative and to the
land management authority or sheriff's department.

WEATHER

Listen to the evening and morning weather
forecasts before departing to get an idea of what to
expect.

Checklists: What You Will Need and May Need on the Trail

This list is predicated on a one- or two-day trip. If you plan a longer hike, be sure to carry enough consumables to cover the extended period.

Essentials—these should be carried regardless of whether you are hiking for one day or one month.
Map
Compass
Extra clothing (warm enough to cover the coldest conditions possible)
Extra food and (if necessary), water
Sunglasses
Plenty of waterproofed matches
Fire-starting kit with either fuel tablets or candle
Pocketknife or belt knife
First-aid kit

Basics
Boots, which you will be wearing
Sleeping bag and pad
Tent, or shelter adequate to house entire party
Waterproof gear
Pack

Other Necessities
Wear clothing suited to the weather conditions the
   day you begin
Food, enough to comfortably feed party during ex-
   pected duration
Stove or cooking tablets
Cooking kit and scour pad
Spoon
Hats (one sun hat and one wool watch cap)
Extra socks, wool outer and nylon inner
Rope (100 feet of quarter-inch braided nylon, pref-
   erably, or at least one-eighth-inch braided nylon).
Toilet paper
Trowel
Handy pack of waterproof matches
Repair kit
Watch
Toothbrush
Soap
Water purifying tablets (if necessary)

Electives
Notebook and pen or pencil
Camera
Light tennis shoes
Sunburn cream
Insect repellent
Chapstick
Fishing equipment

Binoculars
Animal and plant identification books
Down jacket
Towel

Repair Kit
The entire package should be small enough (not larger than a pack of cigarettes), to be easy to carry yet complete enough to handle any minor equipment problem.
Extra shoelaces
Stout thread and needles
Pliobond or other contact cement tube
A small sheet of contact fabric repair material
A small waterproofed nylon drawstring bag to hold
    the materials
Small holes in tents, sleeping bags, or waterproofs can be easily mended with the self-sticking repair tape.

Larger holes should be stitched to bring the edges together, glued over the stitch, and then patched with self-gluing tape.

Holes or rips in packs should be stitched shut and glued-over for a waterproof seal.

A broken tentpole can be mended by fitting a stick between the two halves of the break so that the halves cover the stick, then wrapping the mend with stout sewing thread and gluing over the wrap.

A sole on a boot can be temporarily fixed by cleaning both surfaces (the outer sole and inner sole), with a knife blade and generously applying cement to both surfaces. Clamp with sticks or weight down with heavy rocks until glue has set.

APPENDIX FOUR

Further Reading

I hope *Backpack Hiking: The First Steps* will get you safely and happily through your shakedown hiking trip. It should contain all the information you will need to get your feet decently wet.

But your first trail hike will be, as they say in advertising, a come-on, a way of introducing you to a new world of infinite possibilities. *The First Steps* is designed to get you into the woods and back again with a desire to return to see more and experience more. To do this you will need to know more, and here is a list of books that will help.

THE NEW COMPLETE WALKER Colin Fletcher. A modern classic and one of the reasons so many people are wandering around in the woods these days.

THE MASTER BACKPACKER Russ Mohney. A really excellent advanced backpacker's handbook available in this series.

WINTERING Russ Mohney. Another Packit Book which deals in depth with the specialized equipment and techniques of winter camping.

THE BACKPACKER Albert Saijo. Good source of fundamental lore with an emphasis on "fitting in" the wilderness.

THE WILDERNESS HANDBOOK Paul Petzoldt. Basic backpacking information along with sophisticated mountaineering technique.

MOUNTAINEERING Alan Blackshaw. The ups and downs of mountain climbing around the world.

BASIC MOUNTAINEERING Sierra Club. More down-to-earth than Blackshaw but an excellent book on high mountain hiking and climbing.

BEING YOUR OWN WILDERNESS DOCTOR. Dr. Russel Kodet and Bradford Angier. Basic backcountry medicine.

INDEX